Praise for Cynthia Kane's previous book, *How to Communicate Like a Buddhist*

"Engaging, clear, practical, honest and wise, Cynthia Kane has done a wonderful job illuminating for us a wise path for enhancing communication and relationships in daily life. Start with the people you're most in touch with and just imagine the ripple effects."

— **Elisha Goldstein, PhD.**
Co-founder of The Center for Mindful Living &
author of *Uncovering Happiness*

"Well-organized, easy to digest, and overflowing with nuggets of wisdom."

— **Sasha Tozzi,**
writer, holistic recovery coach & humanitarian

Praise for Cynthia Kane
from former students

"I have noticed numerous changes. The biggest is that more often than not, I am able to pause before thinking and consciously evaluate what I am going to say before I say it! That is a huge deal! In my communication with others, I am also much more aware of when they are responding with default reactions and when they are speaking consciously. I can use these opportunities as learning experiences for my own behavior."

— **Maria J.**

"Awareness changes everything. I became aware of how my emotions and communication are intertwined. Good communication = good emotional health."

— **Luke S.**

"Cynthia's practices have helped me in several ways. I am more confident in my interactions. I have fewer judgments. I am more present in my conversations. I am more patient and tolerant of others. I think more before I speak. I am more silent in conversations and allow others to finish speaking before I talk. I am in a better mood when I speak to people."

— **Colleen R.**

"I was diagnosed with PTSD from my past military service. Now I have the tools to help myself, to feel better about who I am, and to suffer less."

— Misty K.

"I really feel like this content is life-changing for anyone who takes it to heart and puts it into practice. I thought all of the material was very clearly presented with examples and I knew how to apply it in my life right away."

— Matt M.

"The course was life-changing for me. . . The practices Cynthia taught us are so simple yet powerful and easy to integrate into daily life."

— Oliver K.

"I found the information so very relevant and helpful. With these practices, I will always keep discovering and reaping the benefits."

— Ben S.

"Cynthia's practices are such a valuable tool for me. Thank you so much for sharing these gems."

— Carol F.

"I am much more confident in all my interactions. My social anxiety is practically gone! People are opening up to me more and my connections with a wide range of people are growing. I am also getting clearer about my needs and expressing them more effectively."

— Barbara G.

"Well-thought out and not too complicated. It's easy to incorporate the exercises into daily life without too much effort. Results come easily with Cynthia's system."

— Helena B.

Talk to
Yourself
Like a
Buddhist

Patti —
Your words are your power.
I use them kindly.

TALK TO YOURSELF LIKE A BUDDHIST

Five Mindful Practices to Silence Negative Self-Talk

CYNTHIA KANE

Hier⬡phantpublishing

Cover design by Emma Smith
Cover art by Steinar || Shutterstock
Interior Design by Steve Amarillo

Hierophant Publishing
8301 Broadway, Suite 219
San Antonio, TX 78209
888-800-4240
www.hierophantpublishing.com

If you are unable to order this book from your local
bookseller, you may order directly from the publisher.

Library of Congress Control Number:
2017964300

ISBN: 978-1-938289-70-5
10 9 8 7 6 5 4 3 2 1

Printed on acid-free paper in United States of America

Table of Contents

Introduction

There's no denying it, communication is important! In fact, one could easily make the case that communication is central to being human. While other species on this planet can and do communicate with each other, none do so with the complexity and regularity that we do.

Because of this, much has been written about the art of communication, and a trip to your local bookstore will yield a variety of books on the topic, most with a focus on one particular aspect of communication. Some are dedicated to enhancing how we interact in the workplace, others to our romantic relationships, and still more to our relationships with our family and friends.

But all of these books have one thing in common: they are designed to help you learn how to communicate more effectively with *others*. When we talk about communication, we normally think about it in relation to everyone else—only rarely, if ever, do we pay much attention to how we speak to *ourselves*.

As a communication instructor, I find the lack of attention we pay to how we communicate with ourselves alarming, because what I discovered in myself, and confirmed through working with countless clients, is that there is an *unreported epidemic of negative self-talk in our culture today.*

The truth is that many of us speak to ourselves in a way we would never speak to a close friend. Some of us even speak to ourselves in ways that we would never speak to our worst enemy! "I'm so dumb, how could I do that again?" or "I'm such a loser" are common phrases that people say to themselves, but rarely, if ever, do they voice those words to others.

Statements like this are *just the beginning* of how we berate ourselves internally.

In this book I will cover the many often unnoticed ways we talk down to, berate, and chastise ourselves. We will look at the instances of our self-talk that are birthed in animosity rather than goodwill. As a simple example to begin this discussion, think for a moment about how many times you've begun a conversation in your mind (or out loud) with a phrase similar to one of these:

I can't do anything right today.

I'm not where I should be in life.

I'm so stupid.

I'd be happier if I just looked more like . . .

Maybe things would have been different if I had just . . .

I'm so bad at that.

I never get this right.

These are just some of the ways we start negative dialogues with ourselves, often without even realizing that what we are saying is negative (we mistake many of our judgments for facts!). Yet when we speak to ourselves this way, we set a tone for our day and our interactions with others in the world. It's very difficult to enjoy life and experience things like peace, happiness, and goodwill on the outside when we aren't providing it to ourselves on the inside.

The purpose of this book is to bring awareness to the ways that we talk to ourselves—specifically, the *negative* self-talk and the underlying self-judgments that we engage in that cloud our perceptions of ourselves and, by implication, the rest of the world. My hope is that by the end of this book, not only will you be more aware of the negative self-talk that most of us seem to engage in regularly, but you will also be able to spot, identify, and release it effectively.

I have included a set of five practices in this book to help you do just that. I developed these practices based on my training as a communication expert and certified mindfulness and meditation instructor and, just as importantly, my own personal experience.

I call this set of practices the Middle Path of Self-Communication.

Those of you who are familiar with Buddhism will recognize the Middle Path reference, but to those of you who are not, don't worry—the reference will be explained thoroughly in this book.

Quickly defined, the Middle Path is a fundamental principle of Buddhism that advocates bringing moderation and balance to everything that you do. When we have balance, we can see things with clarity. When we are out of balance, our vision and perception become clouded, and this includes how we see ourselves.

In terms of self-communication, an example of being out of balance is when you beat yourself up or berate yourself for making a simple mistake or when you compare yourself to others and decide that you are somehow "less important" than they are. Most of us have had these perceptions from time to time, and they reflect a view of ourselves that isn't true. Everyone makes mistakes, and making one is not a cause for self-flagellation. Everyone on this planet is equal; no one is more important than anyone else.

Bringing balance to your self-communication also includes the practice of another fundamental tenent of Buddhism: compassion.

When we think of compassion, we often think of it as it extends to other people. In fact, Webster's dictionary describes compassion as "a sympathetic consciousness of others' distress together with a desire to alleviate it." The only problem I have with this definition is that it's limited in scope. Most often, we learn to extend this principle outwardly to others without extending it inwardly to ourselves. Compassion is a wonderful quality to cultivate both within yourself and for yourself.

Imagine what your days would feel like if you learned to speak to yourself with compassion, as if you were your own best friend. What would your internal dialogue look like if you spoke to yourself with the same compassion you extend to your closest friends and family? If you're like me and most of my clients, your life would be filled with much more happiness and tranquility. While making this change in how you speak to yourself is not easy, doing so can drastically improve the quality of your life.

That is my other hope for you: that by the end of this book, not only will you have learned how to silence your negative self-talk, but you will also begin to speak to yourself with the same tone of kindness and compassion you would use in discussing something with your best friend.

The Middle Path of Self-Communication is a set of practices to help you do just that. To summarize, this is a path that teaches you how to monitor your internal conversations mindfully and notice when they begin to become tainted by untrue, unhelpful, or unkind beliefs, self-judgments, and the resulting negative self-talk.

The Middle Path of Self-Communication does not encourage you to simply replace negative self-talk with a set of positive affirmations, but rather to begin a balanced way of talking to yourself that relies on kindness, without allowing old and unquestioned beliefs to cloud the language that you use with yourself.

Once you begin to practice the Middle Path of Self-Communication with yourself, you will also have a new method by which you can communicate effectively with others. While the primary goal of this book is to show you how to move away from negative *self*-talk and the underlying judgments that cause it, you'll soon see that these processes and practices can be applied to conversations with others as well.

What to Expect from This Book

We'll start by defining negative self-talk and exposing the various ways it affects our daily lives, as you may be surprised by how often it goes unrecognized. After that we will look at the beliefs and judgments that hide underneath such diatribes, so you can understand their relationship to the dialogues that we have with ourselves.

After we have adequately defined the problem, we will delve into the practices of the Middle Path of Self-Communication: Listen, Explore, Question, Release, and Balance. These five practices are helpful when undertaken as stand-alone tools, but when interwoven and used in succession, they form an effective blueprint for moving away from negative self-talk and toward a path of compassionate communication with yourself.

Each practice has an entire chapter devoted to it, and the purpose is to provide you a fuller, deeper understanding of how you can use them to improve your self-communication habits. It's also important to point out that as with many tools in Buddhism, I refer to these concepts as "practices." The choice of the word "practice" is threefold.

First of all, a practice refers to something that you do rather than just read about or think about. To that aim, many of the chapters will include exercises, and you'll need either a journal or some blank paper in order to complete them. It's very important to go through the exercises so you can better implement and understand the ideas presented. Until you do the associated work, you are unlikely to realize the full benefits of the Middle Path of Self-Communication.

The word "practice" also conveys the idea that this work won't be done perfectly. This is very important to remember, because as you will see, some of our negative self-talk is the result of holding ourselves to impossible standards. You want to be careful that you don't turn your progress on the Middle Path of Self-Communication into a measurement by which you further berate yourself.

Lastly, the word "practice" is meant to convey the idea that the process is ongoing. In my experience, we never "win" the battle with negative self-talk. It will still occur after you finish with this book, but when you apply the practices you find here, it's likely that the number of instances and the effect they have on you will be greatly reduced.

The Middle Path of Self-Communication is like medicine to treat the negativity and suffering that, as you will soon see, is largely self-created. Like most medicine today, it has side effects. Unlike some other medications, though, the side effects to using this style of self-communication include feeling good about your body, feeling secure and safe in your finances, and feeling love and peace in your relationships. It's amazing how many perks you will begin to see when you shift how you speak to yourself.

The other benefit to exposing and releasing your negative self-talk is that it can actually improve your communication and relationships with others. For example, I worked with a woman who berated herself constantly about what she perceived as her inability to succeed in her chosen profession. As she went through the practices in the Middle Path of Self-Communication, she was able to discover the source of this negative self-talk and ultimately release it. She realized that before she did the practices in this book, she would come home every day from work in a bad mood and take her negative emotions out on her partner. When she fixed her thinking and the corresponding dialogue with herself, her relationship with her partner benefited too, as he was no longer subjected to the outbursts that were fueled by her negativity toward herself.

Before we embark on the solution, we first need a better understanding of the problem. As you will see in chapter 1, identifying negative self-talk and all of its manifestations is easier said than done.

What Is Negative Self-Talk and How Does It Manifest in Our Lives?

When I was in the fourth grade, I was introduced to William Shakespeare. While his plays may not have made complete sense to me at the time, his soliloquies stood out. A soliloquy is a speech by a character who is voicing their thoughts aloud, mostly when they are by themselves. A soliloquy reveals the character's innermost beliefs and feelings, but what makes a soliloquy different from a monologue is that no other character can hear what they are saying, whether they are present on stage or not. This is exactly how we are communicating with ourselves all day long—reciting soliloquies.

If you've read any Shakespeare, you may know that many soliloquies bring out the doubts, fears, and insecurities of the characters, often showing a contrast between a public persona and what's actually going on inside the character's mind and heart. And while we aren't characters in one of Shakespeare's plays, our modern-day soliloquies are steeped in the same contexts—much of our internal self-talk is doubtful, fearful, or otherwise negative even if we present ourselves as the opposite.

These self-doubting and fearful soliloquies are good examples of negative self-talk, and in the same ways that they affect and control the lives of Shakespeare's characters, so too do they impact us in our daily lives.

All day long, we're all in near constant dialogue with one person—ourselves. This means that the words we choose have an incredibly powerful effect on how we see the world and ourselves. When this self-talk becomes negative, so do our perceptions of who we are and our place in the world.

Simple statements like "nothing looks right on me today" to the more damaging "I can't do anything right" can affect our day in the same way that dark clouds or rain might affect an otherwise sunny day. For some of us, even times of accomplishment and celebration can be usurped by negative thoughts. For instance, have you ever been congratulated on a job well done, only to downplay your accomplishments or point out the issues with what you've achieved? Thoughts like "Well, it's not perfect but it's a start" to "It wasn't that big a deal" are subtle ways that we denigrate our accomplishments and ourselves through our self-talk.

Even something as simple as getting into the shower and noticing that there's no soap can lead to a hurtful dialogue with yourself. Rather than saying something like, "Oops! No big deal, I'll get it tomorrow," we turn on ourselves in times of simple oversights like this one, moving straight to statements such as "Why didn't I remember to get more soap? How could I be so stupid? Why do I always do this?" The truth is that most of us wouldn't talk to our spouse, our children, our friends, or even our worst enemies in this degrading way, but for some reason, our minds think that it's perfectly fine to wield that kind of negative, hurtful language against ourselves.

If this is how I'm talking to myself in my morning shower, I've already changed how I see the world. My shower, which has the potential to be a rejuvenating and refreshing experience, has suddenly turned my mood to one of frustration and irritation. If my shower has already clouded my mood, imagine what a potential chore breakfast will be, or ironing my clothes, or packing my lunch—and that's before I even make it to work, where I have to interact with other people! Left unchecked, this type of negative self-talk can be a prelude to the statement, "I'm just having one of those days."

This is a simple example of how our self-talk can provide the backdrop for our day, like an internal weather forecast. When the forecast is negative, we are creating the atmospheric conditions for a bad day even before that day has started.

While speaking poorly to ourselves in the shower can set us up for a bad day, repeating "I can't do anything right" to ourselves day after day after day isn't just setting us up for a bad day or week; it's subtly paving the path for us to see our entire life through that lens of "I can't do anything right." If you begin to believe your negative self-talk, or the judgment of "I can't do anything right," your entire life will be affected negatively. If you can't do anything right, why bother applying for a new job? Why go out on that first date? Why would you even ask someone out if you're certain that you'd just muck it up in the end?

And here is another problem in this scenario, perhaps the biggest one of all: many of the people I work with wouldn't have recognized that soliloquy in the shower or the resulting follow-up as an example of negative self-talk. The truth is, we often speak to ourselves in subtle negative ways *without even understanding that we're doing it.* As a result, much of our internal negative self-talk slides past our radar without us realizing the damage we are doing to ourselves in the process.

Of course, other soliloquies are anything but subtle when it comes to negativity. Standing in front of the mirror and harshly criticizing some part of your body would be a common example. Almost everyone has spoken negatively to themselves about an aspect of their physical appearance at one point in their lives. Self-talk around physical appearance may range from "My nose is too big" or "my thighs are too fat" all the way to "I'm ugly and unlovable."

When I first meet with a client, they will sometimes tell me they don't consider this body shaming to be an example of negative self-talk. Rather, they argue that these judgments are "factual." As you will see when we go deeper into the practices, none of these types of judgments are true; *they are all subjective.* In this way, you can see how even our overt self-criticism and the damage it causes can go unnoticed.

Other overt negative soliloquies arise from past life events, usually from the experiences we regret or that have left us with unresolved emotions. Examples include divorce, the loss of a job, failing out of school, the time you betrayed a friend, or when you had a serious financial setback.

Overt negative self-talk can also arise from the experiences we suffered at the hands of others. Rape and sexual assault victims often say they carry a feeling of unworthiness or shame, as do the victims of child abuse and other abusive relationships (this includes emotional, mental, and physical abuse). In addition to giving us fodder for overt negative self-talk, the negative self-talk that can develop out of these experiences can also be subtle, as many of its victims don't often realize all the ways in which they have punished themselves for the actions of others.

Negative self-talk that grows loud enough can not only make for an unhappy daily existence, but if left unchecked, it can lead to other, more serious conditions. For example, if you spend enough time telling yourself that you are a horrible person, that you are unworthy of love and friendship, you may develop a tendency to isolate yourself from others, which can lead to depression, anxiety, and even to incidents of self-harm. In these instances, seeing a counselor or other professional is crucial.

We will look at all of the above examples of negative self-talk and their manifestations throughout this book, but for now I ask that you be open to investigating all the ways negative self-talk can appear in your life, including ways you had not previously considered. That is because, as shown in our previous examples, the ways in which negative self-talk manifests can be both subtle and overt. When it's subtle, many of us can have difficulty spotting it, often because we've grown so accustomed to this dialogue that we no longer notice it.

The Buddhist Connection

Buddhism is often understood as a path to eliminate or lessen the suffering in our lives. We often think that suffering arises from forces beyond our control, with old age, sickness, and death being the examples originally pointed to by the Buddha in his discourse on suffering. But the truth is, we create a lot of unnecessary suffering in our lives long before old age, sickness, or death take their toll, simply by the way we communicate with ourselves.

If my internal soliloquy tells me that everything in my life is in upheaval and nothing is going how I planned it, then this negative picture will be reflected in how I feel and the interactions I have with others, and will shape how I see the world.

More to the point, if I tell myself that my life is miserable, then you guessed it—I'm going to suffer. In fact, I have found that speaking to yourself in this negative way isn't just a cause of suffering, it is suffering itself.

But we can lessen the suffering in our lives right now, by changing the way we communicate with ourselves, and examining the beliefs and judgments that provide the ammunition for our negative self-talk.

From a Buddhist perspective, negative self-talk can be defined as language you use when you communicate with yourself that is unkind, unhelpful, or untrue. It's when you speak to yourself in a way that diminishes your very being. This can be in ways that are big and obvious (like when you judge and berate your body), or little and hard to spot (like when you subtly compare yourself to someone else and decide you aren't "enough").

Negative self-talk is language that promotes suffering. As you will see later in the practices, it is largely based on misperceptions of what is true. Negative self-talk occurs when you speak to yourself in thought, word, or action in a way that leaves you feeling sad, upset, or mad at yourself. In this way, negative self-talk occurs anytime we address ourselves with language that creates suffering in our minds.

Later in this book we will look at practices we can undertake in order to lessen the suffering caused by negative self-talk, but I'd like to briefly discuss where we are headed. In my first book, *How to Communicate Like a Buddhist*, I offered the following litmus test for our words when communicating with other people. While *How to Communicate Like a Buddhist* was designed to help you in communication with others, these questions are also important when communicating with yourself.

- Is what I am about to say to someone else true?

- Is it helpful?

- Is it kind?

It can be very easy to answer these questions when you're in conversation with another person, because you have an opportunity to pause or stop before you speak, but when it comes to communicating with yourself, things get a little trickier.

Because of the rapid succession of thoughts that occur in our minds, most of us do not have that same ability to pause before communicating with ourselves. Because of this, our questions change slightly, reflecting our ability to observe what we are thinking or saying. With this distinction, here are the questions we can ask when evaluating our self-talk:

- Is the language I am using with myself right now true?

- Is it helpful?

- Is it kind?

These questions are our mantra on the Middle Path to Self-Communication.

For convenience, I often refer to our thoughts in relation to self-communication, but this is not the only way we communicate with ourselves. Let's take a moment to examine all the modes we use, as understanding them will better help us identify our negative self-talk in all its manifestations.

The Four Modes
of Self-Communication

The four modes of self-communication are the *how* involved in "how do we communicate with ourselves?" As we begin to define what negative self-talk is, we will also take a look at some examples of how it manifests in each of the different modes. Some of you may be surprised to learn that you have communicated to yourself negatively in a way you did not expect or did not realize. Most everyone does so via the first means—through *thinking*—but the truth is that most of us will employ some if not all of the other three from time to time.

1. Thinking

2. Speaking aloud

3. Body language

4. The written word

Thinking

The most obvious way that we negatively talk to ourselves is with our thoughts. It would be great if all our thoughts were true, kind, and helpful, but in reality they are not. I read somewhere that many of the thoughts we experience throughout the day are repetitive. If this is true, it means that many of us are thinking the same negative thoughts over and over. If these thoughts are directed at ourselves, we are often creating the suffering we are experiencing.

Because thoughts are the number one source of negative self-talk, we will dive deeper into why we have these negative thoughts and where they come from in the chapters that follow. As you will see, most of our negative thoughts are not facts; they are judgments and opinions based on past experiences, beliefs, cultural norms, socialization, and a handful of other factors. The practices that make up the Middle Path of Self-Communication invite us to examine the difference between the thoughts that are fact-based and those that are subjective judgments, and give us the tools to shift our internal worldview to a more evidence-based, balanced stance.

Speaking Aloud

Usually we consider speaking aloud as a mode reserved for communicating with others, but if you've ever talked to yourself when no one was around, you've spoken to yourself aloud.

If you are one of the many people who talks to yourself, my guess is that not everything you have ever said to yourself out loud was kind, truthful, or helpful. There are a few key ways of identifying negative self-talk when you are speaking to yourself aloud. When I work with clients, the first words they notice themselves speaking aloud are usually some form of self-criticism: "I can't believe I just did that!" or "I should know better" or "I ought to be able to do this by now." Other clients of mine have noticed they will outright scold themselves when alone, saying things like "I am so stupid" or other self-deprecating statements.

Another way we can engage in negative self-talk is when we speak to others. This may surprise you, but think about it for a moment. How often have you "confessed" what you really think about yourself to a close friend or confidant? Perhaps you have told a friend "I am such a loser" or "I'm so ugly, no one would want to go out with me." Even if your friend tries to convince you that your statement isn't true, you have already spoken negatively about yourself, and you have heard these words as well.

The next time you find yourself speaking to yourself when alone or about yourself to others, I invite you to bring awareness to what you're saying. Are your words true, helpful, and kind? Or do you speak harshly to yourself? If you find it's the latter, don't beat yourself up for having negative self-talk, thus perpetuating the problem. Simply notice it for now, as becoming aware of it is the first step to change.

Body Language

Many times our body language is a product of what we are thinking or saying; thus, this mode of self-communication is related to the first two on the list. It is important to notice the subtle messages we can convey to ourselves through how we hold and use our body when we are speaking or thinking negatively about ourselves.

For instance, when I was going through my meditation and mindfulness certification, one of the exercises we did was close our eyes and imagine ourselves in a stressful situation, and then watch how our bodies responded to stress. For me, my muscles tightened and I became rigid. My heart beat faster and my breathing was shallow.

After that training, I began to notice how my body behaved when I spoke negatively to myself through thought or aloud. I noticed how I would throw my hands up in the air, shake my head, or sometimes even stomp my feet like a three-year-old when I was self-scolding. I was using my body language to reinforce the negative messages I was sending through my thoughts and words.

Think about how you hold your body when you get mad at yourself, or when you feel insecure, ashamed, fearful, or frustrated. Do you slump your shoulders? Do you look down at your feet? Oftentimes you are holding a pose without awareness of the messages you are sending yourself in the process.

The Written Word

The final way we can talk to ourselves negatively is one that most people don't think of: the written word. The classic New Year's resolution is a fantastic example of this. We start the year excited for our goals, but so often our list of resolutions quickly becomes a yardstick that we measure against ourselves. If we don't reach the results we hoped for, we look at the list and add comments about ourselves that aren't positive.

Other examples include writing to-do lists or reminder notes for ourselves that we leave around the house—take out the trash, empty the dishwasher, fold the laundry. These goals, notes, and reminders I write to myself don't have the warm fuzzy vibe of the notes I write to my husband, which are more along the lines of "I love you, please pick up eggs tomorrow." Often, my notes to myself have a curt or demanding tone, which sometimes comes with six underlines to make sure I don't forget or put off whatever it is I need to do—for example, previously I would leave a note to myself to *"FOLD THE LAUNDRY!!!!!!"* I would *never* leave a note like this for anyone else. The way I talked to myself in notes was as though something terrible was going to happen if I didn't get around to crossing off my entire to-do list. But that's not true. The world is not going to end if I don't pick up the dry cleaning today. No nuclear bombs are going to be dropped if I don't get to the dishes tomorrow.

While goal lists and reminder notes are certainly still essential tools that we can use, I find it helpful to compose my lists and reminders as if I'm writing them for someone else. If I were writing a note for my best friend I would say "Karen, please fold the laundry. Love, Cynthia." So now, instead of my best friend's name, I just put in my own: "Cynthia, please fold the laundry. Love, Cynthia." This sounds simple, but I can tell you it feels so much better to receive a note written with politeness and respect than it does a command—even if the note is coming from myself.

Lastly, for those of you who keep a diary or journals, this can be another place you speak negatively to yourselves, often without realizing it. This was definitely true for me. When I began noticing my own communication habits a few years ago, I turned to my journals and saw statements like "I should be over this by now," and "I'm too emotional, this isn't how normal people handle their emotions." I invite you to go back and look in your own journals if you have them. Are there places where what you wrote to yourself wasn't true? Or helpful? Or kind?

No matter which of the modes of communication we are using to talk to ourselves, the first step to changing negative self-talk is to identify it when it arises. The four modes of self-communication are *how* we communicate with ourselves, and becoming cognizant of all the ways we talk to ourselves about ourselves gives us a better opportunity to catch all the manifestations of our negative self-talk. In the next chapter we will dive deeper into the ways we engage in negative self-talk and identify the beliefs and judgments that support this habit.

Exercise

Look back over the last week and see if you can identify some ways you spoke negatively to yourself and what mode of communication you used.

Here are some simple examples to help you get started:

"I'm so stupid! I didn't get eggs while I was at the grocery store!" —*thought*

"I texted my best friend and confessed about how fat I feel after skipping the gym this morning." —*written word*

"I dropped a plate and yelled out loud, 'That was dumb!' when it broke." —*spoken word*

Key Ideas

- Negative self-talk is the soliloquy or monologue that feeds our doubts and fears, and contains language that is untrue, unhelpful, or unkind.

- Sometimes we have lived with negative self-talk for so long that we don't even know when we're doing it.

- The four modes of self-communication—thinking, speaking aloud, body language, and the written word—invite us to notice all the ways we speak negatively to ourselves.

Judgment: The Accomplice of Negative Self-Talk

As we begin our chapter on the correlation between judgment and negative self-talk, I'd like to share with you a story from the Zen and Taoist traditions.

> *There was once an old farmer whose horse ran away. Hearing that the horse was gone, his neighbors came to visit and commented, "Oh! What terrible luck you're having!"*

"Maybe," the farmer replied.

The next morning the horse came back and brought with it three other wild horses. The neighbors commented, "Oh! How wonderful this is!"

"Maybe," the farmer said.

The next day, the farmer's son tried to ride one of the wild horses, was thrown off, and broke his leg. Again the neighbors came, "Oh! What a horrible accident!"

"Maybe," answered the farmer.

The day after, military officials came to the village to draft young men into the army. Seeing the son's leg was broken, they passed him by. The neighbors congratulated the farmer, "Oh! That worked out so well for you!"

"Maybe," said the farmer.[1]

---

1 This traditional story has been excerpted from *Zen Shorts* by Jon J. Muth, Scholastic Press, 2007.

While there are many lessons to be gleaned from this tale, the important one for our purpose is the subjectivity of judgment. In the story, an event happens to the farmer, then the neighbors judge it to be good or bad. The farmer points out that all of their judgments depend on how you look at things.

Just like the neighbors and their unsolicited opinions, this is how our minds work much of the time. An event occurs and that's a fact, but then the mind makes a judgment about that event, in which it declares the event as good or bad, wanted or unwanted, loved or feared. When the judgment of an event is negative and that event is related to our sense of self, we have now laid the groundwork for the negative self-talk that inevitably follows.

This brings us to a central point about the origin of negative self-talk: it is *always* coupled with a critical judgment that you've made about yourself and your world. The relationship between negative self-talk and judgment is one we will continue to come back to throughout this book; as you will see, they always go hand in hand.

The way in which our mind judges and interprets events is the result of things such as our upbringing, past experiences, societal influences, and basic personality. You will have an opportunity to look closely at your own history with these topics later, but for now, let's take a more detailed look at the relationship between judgment and negative self-talk.

Imagine that you are standing naked in front of a mirror. That is the event: you are standing in front of a mirror, looking at your body. You can see your reflection clearly. But as you stand there, looking, you inevitably begin to focus on your "flaws," or the things about your body that your mind judges to be deficient.

"My stomach is too big," or "My legs are too short," or "My chin is ugly," are judgments that may enter your mind. Instead of just seeing the image in front of you (your body, as it is) without judgment, you now see "flaws" in your physical form instead. This is where the negative self-talk begins; fueled by these judgments, you begin to tell yourself things like "I look fat," or "I look ugly."

The negative self-talk here is pretty obvious, but what isn't always obvious is that these statements are based on our judgments and opinions, and are not "facts" in and of themselves. Beauty and ugliness are all subjective, to start, and besides that, "fat" is also entirely relative. What may be considered overweight for a person of a certain sex, age, and height could be underweight for a different person. There is no hard-and-fast line to base these judgments on, which is exactly why they are just that—*judgments*, not facts.

While we all may have different opinions on beauty and weight, there is one thing we can all agree about: each time we tell ourselves that we look fat, we feel worse about how we look, which causes us to suffer.

Over time, as we integrate this self-talk more deeply into our being, we begin to believe that we are what our self-talk says, and the "I *look* fat" becomes the belief "I *am* fat."

Left unchecked, the mind can create a whole negative narrative around this type of self-talk. "I am fat" can easily become "I am fat, so no one will love me." And our cycle of suffering continues to grow.

For a subtler example, you may find that judgment and negative self-talk originate with something outside of you, like a material possession—let's say your home. Let's pretend for a moment that you really like having a big, flashy house. In some small way we can say you have made your home an extension of your self-image.

If you see a friend, family member, coworker, or even stranger with what you *compare* and judge to be a "nicer" home than yours, you may subtly sneak in some negative self-talk around this judgment. After the judgment, the negative-self talk comes naturally. "If I would just work harder I could afford a home like that," or "If I had taken that new job, not spent so much money on vacation, then I could have had a house like that." Or perhaps your self-talk might go the other way: "I will never be able to afford a house like that."

The event that occurred is that you saw someone else's house. Then judgment came in. You compared their possession to your own and judged that theirs was somehow nicer or better than yours. Negative self-talk was the result.

When we see this type of comparison judgment and negative self-talk on paper, it's much easier to spot the absurdity of this thinking, but when it happens in the mind, it can be quick and insidious.

For those of you who may be having trouble relating to the example of home ownership, you can easily replace this with anything that you envy in others, like a job, a material possession you have made an extension of your self-image, physical appearance, educational background, financial status, and of course even progress on a spiritual path ("I'm not a good Buddhist like that person").

In all of these instances we are equating something outside of us with who we are, and as a result we aren't seeing things clearly. In Buddhist terms, we are experiencing delusion. Delusion is one of what Buddhism calls the three poisons, or the three main causes of suffering (the other two are greed and hate). When we don't see things clearly, we are by definition out of balance.

We are deluded because hidden behind the idea that "my body is not enough," or "my possession is not enough" is the implication that "*I* am not enough." In other words, when you judge that your body, your car, or your "fill in the blank" is inadequate, then by extension you infer that you too are also inadequate. As a result of this feeling of inadequacy, you may notice that you act differently around the person you judge as having a "better body" or a "more successful career" than you, and this is another example of how negative self-talk can affect your views and behavior in the world.

When we buy into our judgments, the negative self-talk only reinforces them, even though *any judgment* itself is by definition not a fact of objective reality, but as in the story of the farmer's neighbors, simply a subjective opinion. Our goal here is to be like the farmer in the story, who wisely surmised that good and bad are simply a matter of perspective.

We will learn how to evaluate our judgments and to circumvent them in the exploring and questioning practices, but for now I would like to focus on what I call the Seven Common Expressions of Negative Self-Talk, which represent some of the most typical judgments and negative self-talk that many of us experience. Learning these categories and the corresponding language they often employ can help you spot and identify negative self-talk as soon as it starts.

Seven Common Expressions

After working with clients and going through this practice myself, I've found that there are seven common categories of expression that include a built-in judgment, each with their own set of buzzwords and catchphrases. These result in some of the most typical ways we speak negatively to ourselves, or in a manner that is untrue, unhelpful, and unkind. By becoming aware of these categories and the buzzwords that are commonly associated with them, you can more quickly identify when your language is coming from judgment and negative self-talk. The seven common expressions are:

- Overreaction: *"Everything* is terrible!"

- Personalization: "Why is this happening to *me?!"*

- Absolute language: "I *am* a bad person."

- Assumption: *"He thinks* I'm not good enough!"

- Expectation: "This isn't how it's *supposed to be*!"

- Comparison: "Why can't I be *like her?"*

- Regret: *"If I hadn't done that . . ."*

Overreaction: *"Everything* Is Terrible!"

Overreaction occurs when we don't see a situation clearly. As it relates to judgment and negative self-talk, overreaction typically occurs after an event happens, when we judge it to be worse than it really is. Examples of this could be making one mistake and considering a whole project ruined, or breaking a promise and judging yourself as an entirely untrustworthy or unreliable person.

For example, a client of mine had been trying to eliminate sugar and processed foods from her diet, but come Halloween, she ate several pieces of candy. Despite having been very strict on her diet previously, after this, my client's self-talk sounded like this: "You totally blew it. There's no point in trying to diet now."

Her judgments exaggerated the facts, and fed that overreaction to her self-talk. Overreaction is a common form of negative self-talk and judgment and occurs when we focus on one aspect of an event and judge it to have far more significance than it actually does; what you are focused on is blown out of proportion, and as a result, you no longer see reality as it is.

Catchphrases:

- Everything is . . .

- Every time I . . .

- This is the worst thing . . .

Personalization: "I'm Responsible for This."

Personalization occurs anytime you believe that what others do and say is a reaction to you. You've likely heard the saying, "The world doesn't revolve around you," but this negative self-talk will make you think just the opposite.

In terms of judgment and negative self-talk, this occurs when we take personal responsibility for the actions of others or for entire situations, and as you can imagine, we judge ourselves negatively in the process. This is often a form of ego, or pride in reverse. The truth is that others are responsible for their own choices, just as we are responsible for ours.

For instance, a client of mine came to me after her divorce because she wanted to improve her communication with her daughter. We discovered that because of the divorce, she felt like all of her daughter's issues at school were her fault. In her mind, *anything* that was going wrong for her daughter was because of the divorce and thus the mother's fault for bringing this upheaval into the daughter's life. The mother judged herself constantly for her daughter's behavior, and when my client started paying attention to her self-talk, she noticed phrases like, "It's all my fault. I know she isn't doing well because of me." Once my client became aware of the "I, me, mine" pattern of her self-talk, she saw how it was causing her relationship with her daughter to suffer and was able to take steps to change her judgments against herself, which greatly improved her relationship with her daughter.

Catchphrases:

- I'm responsible for . . .

- It's *my* fault that . . .

Absolute Language: "I *Am* a Bad Person."

Absolute language expressed in negative self-talk is when we take a description and make it a part of who we are. For example, the true statement, "I have fat on my body," becomes "I *am* fat." Fat is not a person, but simply a part of the body. When you use the absolute language to say that you *are* fat, you are distorting the truth. When you use absolute language, you are ascribing something to yourself and making it you. Instead of being a person who behaved in a manner you now regret, you *are* evil. Instead of being a person with a slightly crooked nose, you *are* ugly. Instead of having less money than you'd like in your bank account, you *are* poor. These judgments can be particularly hurtful because we identify ourselves with them even though they are not clear perceptions of reality. If we tell ourselves we are these things often enough, we start to believe it to the point we mistake these attributes for who we really are.

This can also happen through negation. In other words, "I am not" is just as powerful as "I am." For example, a client came to me wanting to improve how he expressed himself to others. When he contacted me, he conveyed his concerns about his communication style perfectly, despite his long-running negative narrative that said he was not good at expressing himself. Because he accepted this self-imposed label, he shied away from relationships and social interaction for fear that he couldn't talk to people adequately. As he became more aware of the way his self-limiting belief and language were perpetuating the problem, it became easier for him to release the label of "poor communicator" that he had adopted.

Catchphrases:

- I am . . .

- I am not . . .

Assumption: "*He Thinks* I'm Not Good Enough!"

Making assumptions is one of the most common types of judgment that leads to negative self-talk. When we make assumptions, we assume we know what others are thinking or feeling about us, we judge that their thoughts or feelings are negative, and then we berate ourselves because of this judgment. In other words, we actually agree with the assumption we are making, even when it has no basis in reality.

For instance, I had a client who saw her boss at a restaurant one evening after work. He was sitting across the room, and my client waved to him. Rather than waving back, her boss scrunched up his face and gave her what she described as an "evil eye" before returning to his meal. My friend was mortified. She had all sorts of ideas about what this meant, and as you can imagine, not a single one of them was good. For the next few days she wrestled with what the interaction could mean. She engaged in self-talk that said she wasn't doing her job well or that her boss didn't like her (and she used this to justify her own beliefs that she was unlikable). Finally, she went into his office and peppered him with questions: Was her job secure? Was there anything he felt she needed to do better? Did he not like her for some reason? Her boss was surprised at the conversation, and after assuring her that he was happy with her work, he asked what had prompted this concern on her part. My client reminded him about the restaurant encounter from a few days earlier. "Were you there?" he replied. "I'm so sorry I didn't see you, I had just taken my contacts out and I'm as blind as a bat without them." My friend laughed as she told me what her boss said, but the fact that she had spent a few days suffering all based on an assumption is no laughing matter.

This story serves as a good reminder that our assumptions are more often reflective of what we think of ourselves than what anyone else thinks about us, and when we make assumptions, even small ones, they can fan the flames of our negative self-talk.

Catchphrases:

- They think . . .

- They feel . . .

- They did this because . . .

Expectation: "This Isn't How It's *Supposed to Be!*"

Not meeting an internal expectation is one of the biggest ways we create negative self-talk. If we set an expectation for ourselves that we don't meet, few of us say things like, "That's okay, dearest, you did your best and everything will be okay," even though this is almost always how we would speak to our best friends.

Expectation is a common way that we take a positive habit or practice we're involved in and use it against ourselves, and when we do so, negative self-talk is sure to follow. For instance, if you develop a good habit of working out three times a week and then you miss a session, how do you treat yourself? Oftentimes these positive activities can quickly become yardsticks by which we measure ourselves and then berate ourselves when we don't meet our own expectations. In this way, you are causing your own suffering, by converting a positive into a negative.

My friend witnessed an example of this on her mother-in-law Shelley's birthday. Shelley is a successful, retired professional and proud mother of two grown, wonderful sons, but on her birthday this past year she suddenly started sobbing. When asked why she was crying, she said, "I'm sixty-four years old and I thought I would have done so much more by now!"

Instead of looking at the beauty of the life she had created, her expectations had become weapons of war—ones she used against herself. Meanwhile, she had a great life with a loving family just waiting to help her celebrate her birthday. None of that mattered, of course, if she told herself otherwise. That is the power of negative self-talk.

Catchphrases:

- This isn't how I wanted it . . .

- This isn't how it's supposed to be . . .

- I am supposed to be . . .

Comparison: "Why Can't I Be *Like Her?*"

Unlike expectations, which are the goals we put on ourselves, comparisons are based on what everyone else is doing or what we perceive their lives to be like. When we compare ourselves to others, we see something they have or some characteristic they possess and judge ourselves as deficient when we don't measure up. I used an example of this earlier in the chapter with the homeowner illustration. Anytime we compare ourselves to others, we are on fertile grounds for negative self-talk, because there will always be instances where we don't measure up. As with most judgments, comparison can also go the other way, and we may judge ourselves as being superior to someone else in some way, which is an equal form of delusion.

In the modern world we have a new and powerful means for comparison, judgment, and the subsequent negative self-talk: social media. I've had many clients express self-doubt and critical self-talk as a result of comparing themselves to the images of their peers they see on Facebook, Instagram, Snapchat, and the like, where lives seem perfect and everyone appears beautiful. I call this "comparing your insides to someone else's outsides." In other words, if you compare how you feel on the inside to how someone else looks on the outside, you'll always come out deficient. This is another example of how when we compare ourselves to others, we create our own suffering.

Catchphrases:

- I wish I could be . . .

- Their life looks better than mine.

- They have way more than I do.

- They always looks so put together.

Regret: "If Only This Hadn't Happened."

To an extent, feelings of regret are laced through many of the other expressions of negative self-talk. But because regret is so powerful when it comes to generating negative self-talk, we will focus on it specifically. Regret occurs when we look back at our past, at things we did or failed to do, and beat ourselves up for this action or inaction.

"If I hadn't gotten divorced," "If only I had stayed in school," "If I had just taken that job," are some examples of how an expression of regret may start. In other cases, our sense of regret is the result of something that happened to us.

In either case, regret is another instance where our negative self-talk can be quite subtle, because most of us are convinced that this judgment of our past is true. We will look more deeply at this in the practices that follow.

Catchphrases:

- I never should have done . . .

- That will haunt me the rest of my life . . .

- If that had never happened, I would be . . .

These seven expressions aren't the only ways we speak to ourselves negatively, and you've likely noticed that some of these categories can easily overlap or coexist. As you become more educated and aware of negative self-talk, watch out for buzzwords that will help you identify it more quickly.

Another point I want to reiterate is that these common expressions all contain judgments. That's why, as we begin to move into the solution, the Middle Path of Self-Communication, we will link the ending of negative self-talk with the undoing of judgments.

Judgment and the resulting negative self-talk are at the root of our self-communication that is unkind, unhelpful, and untruthful—and this is how we create suffering in our own lives. Silencing our negative self-talk and moving into the Middle Path of Self-Communication are largely a journey of identifying and investigating the judgments we've made over the years and subsequently releasing those that simply aren't true. The exercise that follows will help you get started.

Exercise

What's Your Self-Communication Style?

Just like studying Shakespeare's soliloquies, our own soliloquies can give us huge clues about what we need to work on by seeing which themes come up time and time again. Most people find that one or two common expressions regularly occur in their internal monologues more than others. Here is your opportunity to identify yours.

Write down the phrases that you are repeating in your mind. "I look fat." "I am a bad employee." "I'll never find someone to love me." For now, you don't need to do anything but observe which phrases come up. This will give you more tools to work with when we move into the process.

Key Ideas

- Negative self-talk is always accompanied by judgment. When you notice that you are engaging in negative self-talk, see if you can find the accompanying judgment.

- There are seven common expressions of negative self-talk. Each expression comes with its own catchphrases and buzzwords. Learning these watchwords can help you better identify negative self-talk and judgment when they pop up.

CHAPTER 3

The Middle Path of Self-Communication Overview

So far in this book we have defined negative self-talk and examined the various ways it can arise. We've also discovered that negative self-talk is always accompanied by an underlying judgment. Now it's time to explore five practices we can use to change this—what I call the Middle Path of Self-Communication. In this chapter I will give you an overview of all five practices, and then we will delve deeply into each of the practices in subsequent chapters.

The five practices of the Middle Path of Self-Communication are:

1. Listen

2. Explore

3. Question

4. Release

5. Balance

As we begin down this path, remember that we strive to bring compassion to our internal dialogue, and this means speaking to ourselves using words that are true, helpful, and kind.

Rather than allowing our old patterns of negative self-talk and its underlying judgments to dominate our minds unregulated, we will want to explore and question the words we use with mindful curiosity and the willingness to release any old, outdated beliefs or assumptions we find.

The first step in shifting our negative self-talk is to become aware of it, to recognize when we are engaging in it. That is a crucial component, as much of the negative self-talk we manufacture can go unnoticed. That's why much of the book so far has been devoted to helping you spot and identify negative self-talk in all its manifestations.

Our first practice is to *listen* to what you are saying to yourself throughout the day, but it is particularly vital in times of stress or suffering. I have found that anytime I am suffering, there is a good chance I am speaking to myself negatively in some way too. The goal of listening is to discover where and how you are speaking negatively to yourself, which, as we have seen, can be subtle or overt. I've said this before but it bears repeating: many of us are so used to this hurtful way of communicating with ourselves that we may not even notice when we go into negative self-talk. That is why the practice of listening to yourself is so important: you cannot change what you do not observe.

After you identify that you are engaging in negative self-talk, the next practice is to *explore* where this talk is coming from. This means that you will start to chase down your judgments and the beliefs that support them, as these are always the underlying causes of self-flagellation. These judgments may come from an old wound or a defense mechanism that may have been necessary at one time in your life, but is no longer serving your highest good. When you explore the negative self-talk, you may be able to follow it back to the source of the belief and judgment that gave rise to it in the first place. This allows you to fix the problem at its root. The exploration process also gives you a certain amount of analytical detachment and distance from the self-talk so you can move forward in the process of shifting how you speak to yourself without frustration or fear.

Feeling some detachment from your self-talk gives you the opportunity to *ask questions,* specifically:

- What judgment am I making?

- What story am I telling myself as a result of this judgment?

- What do I know to be true?

Answering these questions can help you see the situation clearly. In many instances, the answers will be eye-openers, and as a result they will serve as your secret weapons against negative self-talk. This practice can be best summed up by the axiom, "the truth will set you free."

The next practice is to *release* old judgments. With the truth as your guide, you can start to let go of old judgments and beliefs and, in so doing, take away the supports that are holding up your negative self-talk. Oftentimes the barrier to releasing old judgments is forgiveness, for yourself, for another, or for a situation. Furthermore, when we practice releasing old judgments, we are attempting to let go, and this includes letting go of our habit of trying to control or change things, especially things that occurred in the past.

The last practice is to strive for a state of *balance.* This invites us to take a steady and truthful view of ourselves and the events of the world, rather than being led about by our judgments and corresponding negative self-talk. Here is where we endeavor to replace our old self-communication habits with new ones and subject each of them to our borrowed-from-Buddhism negative self-talk litmus test: Is what I am about to say to myself true? Is it helpful? Is it kind?

Running through and alongside all of these practices is a sense of compassion, as throughout this journey my hope for you is that you learn to speak to yourself as if you were your own best friend instead of your own worst critic. The truth is that you *are* your own best friend. No one has as much stake in your own mental well-being as you do, and these practices are simply ways to help you act like an invested friend to yourself, rather than a stranger or, worse, an enemy.

With this brief overview in mind, we will now drill deep into each practice one at a time. For many of my clients, these practices require a little time and persistence before they begin to feel the benefits. For most people, negative self-talk has been going on for quite some time, and relief will take time as well.

Key Idea

- The Middle Path of Self-Communication is a set of practices to help you become aware of, investigate, and release negative self-talk and the underlying judgments that you experience.

CHAPTER 4

The Practice of Listening

An accomplished scholar visited the Zen master in order to inquire about Zen.

Offering the scholar a cup of tea, the master continued pouring even after the cup was full. As the tea spilled on the table, the scholar watched for a moment and finally shouted, "Can't you see the cup is full?"

The master smiled, stopped pouring, and replied, "Can't you see that you are like the cup? How can I teach you anything when your mind is so full of ideas? You must empty your cup."[2]

L ike one of the messages in this story, the practice of listening carries with it the willingness to learn something new. When we really listen, we let go of our old *ideas* about the way things are in order to find out how they *actually* are. Our first goal in this practice is to discover how we actually speak to ourselves rather than how we *believe* we do. In other words, many people are surprised at how much negative self-talk they actually engage in once they learn to listen to themselves and notice it in all its manifestations.

As I mentioned earlier in this book, one reason that it's difficult to notice our negative self-talk is because we've learned to live with this kind of self-talk for so long that we mistake our negative judgments for facts. With the tools from the previous chapters, you should have a better grasp on the forms negative self-talk can take, and how it may express itself in your life. In order to employ those newfound skills, we have to start listening to ourselves mindfully.

---

2 Versions of the teacup story appear in many places. For a good explanation of its origins please visit https://www.thoughtco.com/empty-your-cup-3976934.

Mindfulness is a fundamental component of true listening and essential to freeing yourself from old judgments and self-talk. Mindfulness is the practice of being aware of the moment you're in with nonjudgmental attention. What sets mindfulness apart from what we commonly think of as "paying attention" is that with mindfulness, you become an observer or witness of whatever may come up inside of you, and this includes self-talk. Seen in this light, I define mindfulness as paying attention to what's happening in the outside world as well as what is happening in your inside world, all in the present moment.

Oftentimes we don't pay attention to our own thoughts and words or the subtleties of what is going on around us, and it's more accurate to say we are moving about the world on autopilot rather than experiencing the world and our inner dialogue in the moment.

Here is another Zen story that illuminates this issue quite well.

> A man on a horse came galloping
> quickly down the road. It seemed
> as though the man had somewhere
> important to go.
>
> Another man, who was standing
> alongside the road, shouted, "Where
> are you going?" and the man on the

horse replied, "I don't know! Ask the horse!"[3]

For many of us, our mind is like an untamed horse, constantly pulling us down a path of suffering. It uses our negative self-talk and judgment to buck and throw us off balance. The practice of mindful listening is the first step toward taming the horse.

Breathing exercises are particularly good for introducing you to the basics of mindfulness. For example, take a moment right now to inhale a deep, lung-filling breath. Feel the air moving through your nose and down into your lungs. Now exhale, slowly and with complete control of your body. Feel the way the tension in your shoulders eases, how your chest expands with each breath. In this way, you've put your awareness, your mindfulness, on your breath and have tuned in to what is happening in this exact moment.

Mindfulness traces its origin to Buddhist meditation. To be mindful in Buddhist meditation means to witness and observe thoughts without attaching too much importance to them. Our goal instead is to simply let them pass by like clouds across the sky. Many people (perhaps including yourself!) who have meditated previously will likely agree that this is easier said than done.

---

3 This traditional story has been excerpted from *ZEN STORY*: "The Horse (Mindfulness)." Bodyandsoulnourishmentblog, 5 Dec. 2016, amiracarluccio. com/2016/08/31/zen-story-the-horse/.

In our practice of listening, the goal is to bring that same observational mindset expressed in Buddhist meditation to our internal monologue, specifically when it is negative. By noticing the negative self-talk without automatically attaching ourselves to it (that is, believing it) we are already taking a step toward ending it.

Here is where I suggest you start with this practice. Anytime you find yourself feeling sad, angry, guilty, ashamed, afraid, stressed out, regretful, or any other negative emotion, let this be your cue to really listen to your inner dialogue mindfully.

It's often in these moments of suffering, or when things aren't going the way we want them to, that we turn on ourselves. For instance, if you're feeling guilty, ashamed, or regretful, you may notice yourself saying, "If I hadn't done X, Y, or Z, things would be different now . . ." In times of frustration or stress you may notice that you say to yourself, "I just can't do anything right . . ."

Through mindful listening, you may actually find that in some cases, many of the negative emotions you are feeling are the direct result of the negative self-talk, or even when your feelings are not the result of your own internal monologue, it's at these moments that negative self-talk is prone to rise and add fuel to the already burning fire of your suffering.

In either case, the main goal is to no longer let these harmful words and the underlying judgments go by unnoticed and unquestioned, and mindful listening is the key to helping you get there.

A helpful technique to combat negative self-talk is to simply name it as such in the moment. For example, if I hear my self-talk say, "Okay, Cynthia, that's a stupid idea," I reply to myself, "That was negative self-talk." I don't accuse myself or beat myself up for making the statement, I just observe that it was negative. In this way, naming your negative self-talk will help you not attach yourself to it.

Oftentimes just noticing your self-talk and not attaching to it will make you feel better immediately, and in this way your listening practice will be helpful in and of itself. Once the negative self-talk is identified, you can proceed to the next steps on the Middle Path of Self-Communication, either just after you notice the negative self-talk, or later in the day when you have more time for deep exploration. The good news is that just the initial act of being mindful of your negative self-talk can lessen your suffering, because anytime you notice this type of unhelpful communication, it means you are less attached to it.

Bringing Compassion to Your Self-Communication

The next part of our listening practice invites us to bring compassion to ourselves when we notice that we are engaging in self-talk that isn't true, helpful, or kind. In this way, the listening practice is helpful as a stand-alone practice, providing a vehicle for us to act like our own best friend instead of our own biggest critic. I can't overstate the importance of this, as bringing compassion to yourself can change your life immediately by altering the way you feel. It's difficult to stay angry at yourself and bring compassion to yourself simultaneously. Bringing compassion to yourself will also help you support yourself as you move through the rest of the practices.

In many Buddhist circles, compassion is cultivated by seeing the other as yourself. You bring mindful attention to the suffering of others, the pain of others, the wants and needs of others, and in so doing you gain the understanding that others are very much like you. This is a wonderful practice, and most anyone who has tried it can attest to its effectiveness.

When it comes to developing compassion for yourself, I'd like you to do a related (and yet opposite) version of this practice. Instead of seeing others as yourself, I'd like you to see yourself as another—specifically, your best friend.

Take a moment to think of the person you love and care for the most in the world, and then think of all the times you have encouraged and supported them, especially when they were experiencing challenging times. Imagine what you would say to them if you heard them say something like, "I'm such a loser," or "I'm so ugly," or "I failed again."

Now I want you to see yourself in their place and repeat the same words of comfort that you would share with your best friend. Perhaps you would say something like this to him or her: "It's okay, you are doing fine, please stop beating yourself up." I want you to speak these same words to yourself the next time you notice yourself engaging in a negative diatribe.

For most of us, this is a drastic shift in our dialogue with ourselves. We cause so much unnecessary suffering in our lives through the way we speak to ourselves. Mindfully listening to negative self-talk and replacing these words with compassionate language instead can alleviate or at least lessen much of this suffering.

As a side note, one of the reasons that self-compassion is so difficult is that society often affirms the opposite, even going as far as celebrating self-compassion as a weakness rather than strength. For instance, my local gym offers a fitness class they call "boot camp," and that's not surprising when you consider how many of us bring a drill sergeant mentality to accomplishing our goals, especially in the areas of diet and fitness. Our language also supports this type of thinking, as there's a well-known sentiment in our society that it is desirable to "pull yourself up by your bootstraps" when you are in a difficult situation, rather than relying on help from an outside source. While I have nothing against getting in shape or accomplishing goals, I hope you notice that what's implicit in these messages is the idea that you need to whip yourself in order to get there.

This begs the question: is all this self-flagellation really necessary to accomplish goals? Is it possible to get just as much done while cheering yourself on? In my experience the answer is that in fact, the cheerleader approach is even more effective than the drill sergeant, and it certainly makes for a happier existence during the process.

The Negative Self-Talk Trap

Mindful listening can also help you from falling into the trap of "beating yourself up for beating yourself up." In other words, some of my clients, as they begin to notice their negative self-talk, start berating themselves for having self-talk at all, telling themselves something like, "I can't believe I have all this negative self-talk and I never even realized it! What's wrong with me?" or "I can't believe that even after having read the book and taken her course, I am *still* beating myself up!"

This is an example of how more negative self-talk can sneak in the back door. We use tools meant to help us as measuring sticks to hurt us, and we beat ourselves up if we don't practice perfectly. Be careful of this as you move forward in this journey.

Knowing how to mindfully listen to ourselves means we can start paying more attention to the ways we talk to ourselves negatively, knowing now that the goal is not to criticize, analyze, or become angry or disappointed at ourselves for it, but to simply observe and bring compassion to ourselves instead. For instance, rather than the above statements, we may say something like, "I see that I'm speaking negatively to myself in this moment. I'm glad I noticed it. I'm still learning and I'm doing my best."

My point here is to go easy on yourself as you begin to undertake this practice, as for many people it represents an entirely new way of interacting with yourself. The goal here is to no longer live on autopilot, letting your mind drag you around the way an untamed horse would, and to meet its negative pronouncements with compassion instead. Once you have done this, you can turn your attention to the practice of exploring the underlying beliefs and judgments that give rise to your negative self-talk in the first place. That is the focus of the next chapter.

Exercises

Becoming Mindful of Your Personal Preferences for Negative Self-Talk

I've found through my own experience and working with clients that while we can have some level of negative self-talk in any area of our lives, most of us have "themes" or preferred areas that we regularly return to with our negative self-talk. Below are some common categories and examples of what negative self-talk might look like in each. After reviewing them, make a list of your own categories. It may be helpful to look at the list you made in the previous exercise about identifying your own repetitive self-talk.

Feel free to alter these categories to suit your individual needs (for example, some people may choose to split the *relationships* grouping into *spouse* and *family*, depending on the self-talk they have around each).

If you are having trouble coming up with instances of when you experienced negative self-talk, start by remembering a time when you were suffering, and then try and remember the corresponding self-talk from that moment. You can also use your list from the previous exercise to get you started.

Relationships

I am unlovable.

I am unappreciated.

No one loves me like they love her.

I'll never find true love.

I'm a bad partner/son/daughter/family member.

Physical appearance

I am ugly.

This outfit is the worst thing I could wear.

I feel gross.

I'm not as attractive as him/her.

Work/education/finances

She is more successful than I am.

Wow! I'll never afford a house like that.

I'll never get where I want to be because I never finished college.

I'm lousy with money.

Personal development (progress on a spiritual path, hobby, etc.)

Their art is so much better than mine!

I've read all the books, I should be enlightened by now.

I meditate daily, but I still get angry in traffic. What is the matter with me?

Fire the Drill Sergeant, Hire the Cheerleader

The drill sergeant is an icon for suffering in our culture, yet many of us wake him up for duty every morning. This is an invitation to dismiss the sergeant and replace it with a section of cheerleaders instead. Start by listing any areas in your life where you push yourself with a drill sergeant mentality—likely candidates are dieting, exercise, and work-related goals. Now, the next time you begin a task associated with this area, speak to yourself as if you were your best friend just before you begin and then again when you end.

A friend of mine is an avid tennis player and experienced some wonderful benefits when he undertook this exercise. By listening to his thoughts as he played, he noticed that when he made a bad shot he would often scold and yell at himself, saying "Come on, Ben! Get it together!" or "That shot was terrible, what's the matter with you?" For two weeks he made a conscious effort to replace that language with more positive statements when he made an error, saying instead "That's okay, you'll do better next time," or "Relax a little, and let it flow."

He feels like this change not only improved his game, but also made the time playing far more enjoyable! I invite you to experiment with your own cheerleading statements once you fire your drill sergeant and see if you experience similar results.

Key Ideas

- The practice of listening helps us to notice our negative self-talk and allow it to drift away without our attaching to it.

- As you listen to yourself, try to bring compassion to yourself when you notice you are speaking to yourself unkindly.

CHAPTER 5

The Practice of Exploration

One of the things I love about Buddhism is that it's realistic. Rather than having a rule that says "don't judge," Buddhism accepts and understands that judgment often occurs in the mind whether we want it to or not, and that it's far more helpful to examine the origin of our judgments and see what beliefs we are holding that are supporting these judgments and giving rise to the subsequent negative self-talk.

This is where the practice of exploration comes in. We want to explore the beliefs and judgments that are hiding just underneath our negative self-talk, because these are the root cause of the disparaging things we say to ourselves. Exposing and undoing them can take us a long way toward alleviating unnecessary suffering in our lives.

Most explorers set out to find and reveal truth, and that is exactly what we want to do here. Without this practice we'd be able to notice our negative self-talk and that would be helpful, but this practice invites us to go further. Our goal in this practice is to find out what beliefs or ideas we are holding that are giving rise to negative self-talk and judgment. In other words, we want to find the source.

Here is a wonderful Zen story that illustrates the connection between beliefs and judgment.[4]

> *There was a person coming to a new village, relocating, and he was wondering if he would like it there, so he went to the Zen master and asked: "Do you think I will like it in this village? Are the people nice?"*
>
> *The master asked back: "How were the people in the town where you come from?" "They were nasty and greedy, they were angry and lived*

---

4 This story has appeared in several places, but this version is recounted by Caludia Altucher and can be found at https://thoughtcatalog.com/claudia-azula-altucher/2013/04/8-zen-master-stories-that-illustrate-important-truths/.

for cheating and stealing," said the newcomer.

"Those are exactly the type of people we have in this village," said the master.

Another newcomer to the village visited the master and asked the same question, to which the master asked: "How were the people in the town where you come from?" "They were sweet and lived in harmony, they cared for one another and for the land, they respected each other and they were seekers of spirit," he replied.

"Those are exactly the type of people we have in this village," said the master.

As this story illustrates, we often see what we believe we will see. Consequently, if we don't explore our beliefs, we will continue to see things the same way, make the same judgments, and give rise to the same negative self-talk.

In my experience, there are three primary spheres of influence the mind uses to form beliefs, make judgments, and in turn generate negative self-talk. The three spheres are past experiences, societal ideals, and the concept of scarcity. While these are by no means the only sources, everyone I have ever met has been affected by these spheres to some degree or another. Furthermore, each of these spheres of influence can be particularly potent when it comes to providing ammunition for negative self-talk. As we look closer at these three categories of influence, consider how they have shown up in your own life, specifically in the formation of beliefs that are untrue, unhelpful, and unkind.

Past Experiences

In Buddhism, we often note the relationship between cause and effect. In terms of our beliefs about ourselves, we can say that every action (or inaction) in our past has influenced how we see ourselves in some way. While we all have proud moments, we also carry painful ones—the experiences where we felt unworthiness, guilt, or shame. If we don't consciously deal with the effects of these experiences, we will carry this emotional pain with us, allowing it to form lasting beliefs about who we think we are.

The truth is that every one of us has done things in our lives that we aren't proud of, such as cheated in a relationship, lied to a friend, gotten into legal or financial trouble, become involved in a physical altercation, and so on. If we don't deal with the emotional pain of these experiences in a healthy way, the memories of them will resurface and fuel our negative self-talk.

Similar experiences, perhaps where we judge ourselves as having "failed," can have the same effect on what we believe about ourselves and in turn how we speak to ourselves. Things like getting a divorce, dropping out of school, losing a coveted job, or not getting that promotion are all examples of events that can change how we judge ourselves. We can all look to some event in our past where we experienced disappointment in ourselves, either because of something we did or something we didn't do. One thing all these actions or inactions have in common is that we carry the burden of them around like a weapon and bring it out every so often to beat ourselves up.

For instance, I had a client who left college early in order to take his "dream job." As it turned out, that job didn't pan out as he had hoped, and rather than going back to school, he said to himself that he would return later. Soon thereafter he got married and had a child, and it wasn't long before returning to college was no longer a realistic option. As the years went by, he beat himself up for not finishing his degree, often comparing himself to others in business settings, and was embarrassed to admit he had dropped out of college. The truth was that no one else likely gave it much thought, but my client did, and he labeled himself as "less than," "a failure," and "a quitter" every time he did so.

Shifting gears for a moment, there are also those experiences in your past when you were the recipient of someone else's wrongdoing, and their actions continue to make an impact on how you see yourself now. If you were abused (as a child or as an adult), regardless of whether that abuse was physical, mental, or emotional, you could unwittingly make it a part of your own negative self-image. Put another way, you could actually form the mistaken belief that you *deserved* the abuse you received. Of course nothing could be further from the truth, but sadly this is so prevalent that entire books have been written on it.

This is also the case for victims of sexual assault, especially in a culture that shames them for coming forward, as so many cultures today still do. If you are the recipient of such a level of abuse, I encourage you to seek additional help from professionals. The practices described here can be a wonderful complement to therapy and associated self-help groups.

Many of us have not experienced victimization at this extreme level, but that does not discount the impact of the victimization we did receive. For instance, a client of mine recounted this story:

When I was in the sixth grade, a group of boys made fun of me. I don't remember their words exactly, but the gist was that I was fat. Before this time I don't ever remember thinking I was fat or even thinking about my body image. But after this point, my perception of myself completely shifted and I began to criticize what I saw in the mirror, judge any outfit I put on, and compare myself to my friends. Before I knew it, twenty years had gone by and I realized that I had allowed this experience to shape my perception of my body for two decades. As silly as it now sounds, the way I saw my body as an adult was in part defined by a group of sixth graders who called me fat. Over the years the details of the story faded to the background and all I was left with was the same self-commentary; "Nothing looks good on me. If I could just lose ten pounds. I'm too fat."

When my client started the practice of exploration, she realized that at least in some small way, she had agreed with the judgments of these boys, and because of this she no longer needed them to be physically present in order to be judged and labeled fat—she took care of that all by herself. For the next several years she judged herself in place of those sixth grade boys whose names she didn't even remember. By her own admission, her judgments and negative self-talk took the reins and did a much better job of putting her down than those boys ever did! That's the power of letting beliefs and judgments form without exploring them.

The good news in her case is that this is where the story changed. By using the practice of exploration, she was able to ascertain one of the root experiences that resulted in this negative self-talk. Her subsequent realization came with almost lightning-strike clarity: my client said that if she didn't want to think she was fat anymore, the first step for her was to no longer agree with those sixth grade boys! As simple as it was in theory (and admittedly much harder in practice), this was an important step in changing her opinion of herself.

It may seem strange that a small judgment of being overweight from twenty years ago could be so significant in your current beliefs, judgments, and the resulting negative self-talk, but this is the power of past experiences, and it's why we do the practice of exploring them.

Societal Influences

Have you ever watched the TV show *Mad Men*? For those of you who don't know, it follows a story set in the 1960s about an ad agency in New York. I was fascinated by the product pitches portrayed in the series—an ad agency could take a product like panty hose and turn it into a must-have for women everywhere or transform a watch into a luxury item for men.

When I was younger, I set up an internship at a local ad agency in Columbus. What I quickly realized was how much creative thinking lies behind this industry. You had to have an incredibly big imagination to come up with stories that would inspire others to want a particular product, especially one that wasn't very pleasant in and of itself (smoking is a good example of this). The story behind almost every campaign was designed to make its viewers feel that the advertised product could make them like the person in the ad: beautiful, successful, desirable.

Although I didn't pursue a career in it, what I took away from my study of advertising was that the messages I was seeing on television, on billboards, and in magazines were all manufactured. These situations and scenes were invented to sell a product or a service based on the ideals of what makes beauty, luxury, health, sex, relationships, and family. Sure, at one level I knew this before I took the internship, but seeing it firsthand had a profound impact on me and made me more aware of the way advertisers use manipulation and story to convince us that happiness is just around the corner, if only we would buy the advertised product.

Other ideas of "success" came to me from movies and TV shows. Because I love watching romantic comedies, I drew messages from them that said that men were supposed to go to extremes to win over the girl, that they were supposed to constantly show their adoration and appreciation; I also learned that men were the ones who were supposed to crave sex more than women and that no Hollywood romantic hero was going to want me if I was a bore or a nag—I had to be interesting, charming, funny, and sexy, and he had to be a superhero, willing to go to any length necessary to win my affection. If a boyfriend didn't live up to the expectations set up by what I saw in movies and on TV, I berated myself because obviously I was not cute enough, interesting enough, sexy enough, or "fill in the blank" enough. Even though some of those ideas disappeared as I grew up, I have found in myself and in my clients that old ideas die hard and can resurrect themselves in new ways if we don't continue to be mindful of their lasting impact.

One problem with living our lives this way is that there is no one-size-fits-all for any of these things. Physical beauty is subjective; healthy relationships mean different things to different people; what you find romantic, or sexually pleasing, is likely different from others. If we accept societal ideas about these things without finding out what is true for us, suffering is sure to follow in the form of self-judgment and negative self-talk.

To be clear, the problem is not that we enjoy movies, TV, or advertisements but that we use these fictitious stories as a ruler to judge real-life situations against, often without knowing we are doing it. Left unexplored, society's ideas of what it means to be happy, healthy, or fulfilled can generate lots of judgment and negative self-talk when we don't measure up to these impossible standards.

Of course professional advertisers are just one example and by no means the only mechanism in society that influences us. Another is the culture we grew up in, with its inherited ideas about good and bad, right and wrong, success and failure. As we grew up, we adopted many of these same ideas without question, and when we didn't live up to them, we had yet another yardstick with which to judge ourselves.

Many of our beliefs and judgments from past experiences come from our childhood and teenage years, when we experienced things for the first time. Some of my clients think that because those experiences were so long ago, they aren't relevant in their lives today. But the truth is that when we were kids, we were like sponges, absorbing every experience and ultimately forming the person we are today.

The society we grew up in has greatly influenced our ideas and beliefs about the world. As a result, it's impossible for any one of us to come to a job or a relationship (be it with family, friends, or a romantic partner) without a preconceived perception of what a family, job, or relationship is "supposed" to look like. If we have preconceived notions about "how things should be" and we don't live up to our part in them, we have unwittingly created fertile ground for self-judgment and accompanying negative self-talk.

For example, a client in her forties had lived with extreme negative self-talk for years, and after exploring her own beliefs in practice with me, she was astounded at how much of a role societal influences had in her own critical self-judgment and negative self-talk. When she was young, she was the opposite of all of the neighborhood girls—she was not athletic or outgoing; for the most part she was shy and a bookworm. She did not go out for cheerleading, nor play softball, nor was she involved in the church groups many of her peers joined. She didn't like those activities, but always felt as though society (and particularly her parents) wanted her to be like the other girls at school. As a result, she tried many of these things to please her parents, even though she had very little interest in them herself.

Without knowing it at the time, she had adopted a role of "people-pleaser," in which she would take up things she didn't want to do just to please her parents and later her friends. Finally, in her forties, she became aware that anytime she disappointed others, she judged herself harshly for it. Her people-pleasing had become so extreme that if she couldn't make others happy, she castigated herself. When she looked deeply at this, she felt that she needed to please others in order for them to love her. She traced this feeling all the way back to her childhood and the belief that if she didn't "fit in," other people, including her own parents, would no longer love or accept her.

Through the process of exploration she realized that it was her job to make herself happy, just as it is others' job to make themselves happy. This realization wasn't fueled by self-centeredness, but rather moving to a place of balance. My client still enjoys being helpful and enjoys making others happy; the difference is she will no longer sacrifice herself in order to do so. This was one of the immediate benefits of exploring her self-talk.

When you start asking yourself what you have learned from society about gender roles, relationships, ideas about physical beauty, financial success, and so on, you can then explore and find out if any of these beliefs aren't true for you. You may realize, as many of my clients have, that a lot of your negative self-talk comes from outside pressure to be something other than what you are or what you really want to be. In short, your judgments and the corresponding negative self-talk are the result of trying to be something you don't want to be, and oftentimes just realizing this will help you let it go.

Scarcity

As we saw in the previous section, society is constantly sending us messages about who we should be and what we should have in order to be happy. Another message that comes in tandem with these is a concept referred to as scarcity, or the belief that there is only a limited amount of what we want, and as a result we better get ours before someone else does. The belief in scarcity is so prevalent in generating negative judgments and self-talk that I want to dedicate some time to discussing it by itself.

While scarcity may or may not have some practical benefits in terms of understanding macro- and micro-economics, in my view it is entirely unhelpful when it comes to most of what we seek in our individual lives. Specifically, the moment we believe that there isn't enough love, or friendship, or material possessions to go around, we begin to see the world through the lens of comparison and competition. When this happens, our fellow humans become our competitors in our quest for more of what we think we need to be happy.

This belief in scarcity fuels another one of Buddhism's three poisons—greed. As we covered earlier in this book, the three poisons—hate, delusion, and greed—are what the Buddha taught was the source of all human suffering. Implicit in our search for more is the belief that we are not enough as we currently are, and this belief creates the perfect atmospheric conditions for negative self-talk.

Sometimes my clients have trouble seeing scarcity as a fiction. "But it is true," they tell me, "there isn't enough to go around." I ask them to look deeper and answer this question: "Have you ever not gotten exactly what you need?"

In other words, while there have been many times in our lives when we didn't get what we *wanted*, when we look back over the course of our lives, the truth is that most of us have always gotten exactly what we needed, even if we didn't think so at the time.

Regardless of whether you agree with me on that point, I think we can all accept that self-talk that arises from a place of scarcity is based on fear, and when you believe that you aren't enough, or that you won't have enough, then negative self-talk isn't far away. Until we examine any belief we have in scarcity, our negative self-talk keeps reminding us of what and who we aren't and what we don't have.

This is why I often ask my clients, have you had *enough* of "enough?" In other words, the word "enough" is a red flag for me; anytime I hear myself say that word, it's a cue for me to see if any judgments around my belief in scarcity are arising in the moment. I can then look more deeply and explore what kind of scarcity I'm experiencing—Is it around finances? Love? Beauty? Once I've identified it, I can remind myself of its inherent fallacy.

You see, a fundamental tenet of Buddhism is that you are enough, you have always been enough, and you will always be enough, exactly as you are. I agree wholeheartedly with this position, and the practice of exploration invites us to see this inherent truth anytime our thinking tells us otherwise.

The Origin of Self-Judgment

Like the seven common expressions, you've probably noticed that the three spheres of influence can also overlap one another, as our past experiences, societal influences, and scarcity come together to form some of our beliefs about what it means to be human.

Another belief that seems to be central to many of our other self-judgments is the idea that "I am flawed, guilty, or unworthy in some way." While a full discussion of this concept is beyond the scope of this book, it's important for us to shine a light on this theme so that we can pay attention to how it comes up in our lives.

First of all, the idea that we are flawed is an ancient one and present in the creation stories of almost every major religious tradition. In the Judeo-Christian and Islamic traditions, we have the Garden of Eden story, which implants in our psyche the ideas of original sin and falling from grace. In the West, where Christianity is the dominant religion, the concept of unworthiness is reinforced through the belief that Jesus came to die for our sins.

Even Buddhist legend recognizes the existence of the "unworthiness" of mankind as part of the human condition. When the Buddha sat under the bodhi tree during his quest for enlightenment, he was visited by Mara the tempter (a Buddhist version of the devil), who tried to dissuade him from continuing his quest by reminding him that he was "unworthy" of enlightenment.

None of this is meant to be an indictment of any of these religions or their ideas—my point here is to simply show that it's very likely you grew up in a society that broadly shares the belief that most people are somehow fundamentally flawed or "unworthy." In some cases, this belief is also a "birthright," because it is based upon the "sins" of our forefathers.

When you step back from this type of thinking for a moment, you can begin to see its absurdity. It is often so ingrained in our minds that it will continue to manifest throughout our lives, and that is why we have the practice of exploration: to see the origins of our own negative self-talk and the judgments and beliefs that give rise to it.

As we come to the end of this section, I would like to make an analogy to medicine. Negative self-talk is the symptom of a great disease (or, as I like to say, the opposite of ease or balance: dis-ease). Our judgments and beliefs are really making us sick. The step of exploring allows us to look at the symptoms we're exhibiting and focus on curing the underlying sickness. The exercises at the end of this chapter are designed to help you do exactly this.

Exercises

Pinpoint Practice

In your journal, pinpoint at least five to ten major experiences in your life. These should be events, interactions, or situations that really affected how you saw yourself as a person in the world. These are the moments when in your mind you went from a good person to a bad person, a caring person to a selfish person, someone lovable to unlovable. Name the experience and add the self-talk and judgments that you heard when you experienced that event. What phrases have you heard yourself say that directly relate to these experiences?

For example, some of these moments might be "when I went through my divorce," "when I experienced the death of a loved one," or "when I cheated on my partner." Maybe when you were going through your divorce, you were overwhelmed with emotion and you said or did things that were unkind or selfish. Perhaps when you and your partner were experiencing difficulties, you broke the monogamy of your relationship and experienced guilt and shame for this mistake. Or when your mother was dying, you got frustrated and angry with her and now feel as though that was her last impression of you. For these examples, I've listed some possible self-talk that might arise, but as always you should write down what resonates with you and what you have found to be true in your experience.

During my divorce, I was unkind and selfish to my former partner. My self-talk about this event is, "You are such a bitch! No one will ever love you again! You are a failure."

....

While my mother was dying, I snapped at her when I was frustrated. My self-talk around this event is, "I am an ungrateful daughter and I am unworthy of her love."

....

When my partner and I were having difficulties, I cheated on them. My self-talk around this event is, "I am untrustworthy and unworthy of love. I don't deserve love or trust now because I betrayed my partner."

....

Because of my traumatic childhood, I have trouble trusting others. "My father/mother deserted me when I was young, and I have trouble with intimacy as a result. That's why I am alone now."

We will work with these further in the next practices, questioning and releasing, but for now I'd like to remind you to bring compassion to yourself once again. As you will soon find out, many of the judgments we make about ourselves simply aren't true.

Exploring the Spheres That Have Influenced You

Look at the list of negative self-talk you made previously in the listening practice (I told you it would come in handy!). Now take this time to explore the judgments and beliefs that support each item on the list. As you do so, take note of what spheres of influence are at play in your judgments and beliefs. In your journal, rewrite the negative self-talk statement, then underneath it write the judgment and belief that supports it. Here is an example:

> Negative self-talk: I'm not as attractive as him/her.
>
> Judgment: My physical features are not enough.
>
> Belief: My body does not fit the societal standards of beauty that are shown on TV and in movies; therefore I will never be as happy, fulfilled, or successful as those people either.

Key Ideas

- By definition, judgments are not facts. They are merely perceptions colored by other influencers.

- Rather than trying not to judge, commit to discovering the origin of your judgment and any beliefs hiding underneath it.

- When you notice yourself engaging in negative self-talk and judgment, see if you can find out where the judgment and underlying beliefs are coming from. Likely spheres of influence are past experience, societal influence, or scarcity.

CHAPTER 6

The Practice
of Questioning

Before we begin the practice of questioning, let's do a brief recap of what we have covered so far. We began our journey by looking at what negative self-talk is and defined it as the act of communicating with ourselves in a way that is untrue, unhelpful, and unkind. We also examined the overt and subtle ways negative self-talk can manifest and explained that this negative diatribe is always linked to a corresponding judgment.

We then introduced a practice of listening mindfully, which helps us to spot and recognize our negative chatter when it occurs and in all its manifestations.

Next we became explorers of our own minds to take a close look at the beliefs and judgments that gave rise to our negative self-talk in the first place.

To an extent, the practice of questioning works hand in hand with the practice of exploration, as here we will learn how to apply specific questions when negative self-talk arises. The practice of questioning is helpful because oftentimes the act of exploring the origins of our negative self-talk, judgments, and beliefs does not give us the full relief we seek. Our purpose in this practice is to go deeper, and the questions we will ask ourselves are designed to help us identify the specific judgment underlying the negative self-talk, pinpoint any story we are telling ourselves as a result of this judgment, and finally focus on what is actually true for us instead.

Here is one of the more famous parables[5] of Buddhism, which can give us further insight into the reason for the questioning practice:

> *A man and some companions were*
> *walking down a country road*
> *when suddenly the man was struck*
> *in the stomach by an arrow. His*
> *companions rushed to his side, and*
> *seeing the seriousness of his plight,*
> *prepared to transport him to a*
> *doctor.*

---

5 This is a retelling of the parable of the poisoned arrow, one of the most well-known teaching stories in Buddhism.

"Stop," the man said to the surprise of his companions. "I will not allow this arrow to be removed until I know more about the man who shot it. What is his name? Where does he come from? What is the name of his family? I also want to know more about the arrow. Is it made of oak or sycamore? Does the point contain poison? If so, what kind of poison?"

His friends quickly realized that he would die from his wound before knowing the answers to these questions.

This story can be understood on many levels, but for our purposes we will focus on one profound truth: human beings are story-making creatures. Our desire to tell stories about the events we witness is one of the strongest habits of the human mind. Rather than just look at and deal with the facts as they are, our tendency is to create complex narratives around the situations that we perceive. Like the man who was shot by the arrow, we often do so to our own detriment. In other words, instead of focusing on the facts and relieving our suffering (removing the arrow), we can get bogged down in the story of the event instead.

For instance, earlier in the book I mentioned a client who saw her boss at a restaurant one evening after work. When he didn't wave back to her, she began to spin an entire narrative around what that could mean: he didn't like her, she was a bad employee, he was likely going to fire her, etc. This story she created had nothing to do with the facts, but she suffered for days until she finally spoke to her boss and found out the truth, which was that he simply hadn't seen her. Although the story she created was completely false, because she believed it without question her suffering continued to grow.

This happens to the best of us. Once we are engaged in negative self-talk and judgment, our minds get on a treadmill of negative thinking. The mind continues coming up with more and more stories that keep us stuck in one place, which only adds to our suffering. Our goal with the practice of questioning is to untangle the facts of reality from any make-believe story we are telling ourselves about them. When we are engaged in negative self-talk, it's often our created story that isn't true, and believing our untrue stories is what makes our suffering worse.

When it comes to asking questions, just like the man who was shot by the arrow, most of us are asking the wrong ones. That's not surprising when you examine how society teaches us to ask questions. For instance, I went to an all girls' school, where I took etiquette classes. This is where I learned to twist empty sugar packets so they looked like bows, which fork to use and when, and how to engage in the art of polite conversation.

It was explained to me in this class that the most important technique to create a good conversation was to ask questions to engage the other person. For instance: What do you do for a living? What are your hobbies or interests? How are you feeling today? I found it revealing that while we are encouraged to ask these questions of others to get to know them better, most of us aren't taught to ask ourselves questions.

It's important for us to ask good questions about our own beliefs and judgments, as well as the resulting negative narrative we create from them. If we do not, the ideas and opinions they represent can fly right past our radar and be accepted as facts. Certainly some of us have asked ourselves questions, as in my own case two of the questions I regularly asked myself were "Why can't I get this right?" or "Why do I always find myself in the same bad situation?"

Of course these aren't the types of questions we're looking for, as the very judgment and negativity we are attempting to evaluate are built into them. The questions we want to ask should help us check the validity of our beliefs, judgments, and the corresponding stories we create from them. Along with mindfulness, this type of questioning is actually a very ancient practice.

Halfway around the world from the Buddha, the Greek philosopher Socrates made a now famous proclamation, "The unexamined life is not worth living." He taught that the practice of asking questions was what helped students to examine and determine the legitimacy of an idea, and this technique of questioning even earned a name: the Socratic method. There are many stories of Socrates asking questions of others in an effort to discover the fallacies and assumptions in their thinking and to determine if what they believed was the truth or not.

This is also our goal with this practice.

Three Revealing Questions

Anytime you hear yourself engage in negative self-talk, I invite you to ask yourself the following questions in rapid secession:

1. What judgment am I making?

2. What story am I telling myself as a result of this judgment?

3. What do I know to be true?

To demonstrate how to use this method of questioning effectively, let's look at a simple example of negative self-talk and see how it applies in the situation.

A client of mine saw on social media that some of her friends were coming to her hometown for a gathering, but none of these friends had asked her to join. Her self-talk went something like this: "Nobody wants to hang out with me; they don't really like me . . . I wonder why they don't want to include me? There must be something wrong with me."

As you can see, she created a whole internal narrative of why she was undesirable, and soon she was stuck in a cyclone of negative self-talk. When she became aware of her negative self-talk, she started the unraveling process by listening to what she was saying and then asking herself questions about the judgments and narrative behind it.

Question #1: What judgment am I making?

By now you know that anytime we engage in negative self-talk there is always a corresponding judgment right behind it. The first step is identifying that judgment so you can examine it more closely.

In response to the first question, "What judgment am I making?," my client wrote down that because her friends did not invite her to attend their gathering, she judged that this meant that they did not like her, and because of this she further judged herself as undesirable and unwanted.

Question #2: What story am I telling myself as a result of this judgment?

The second question acknowledges our story-making tendencies, and supports the idea that it's not what happens that causes our suffering, but rather what we tell ourselves about what is happening that keeps us stuck in pain and drama. Situations occur, but it's the judgment and accompanying story we tell ourselves that often create the "problem." Our minds spin an entire negative narrative as a result of the judgment and negative self-talk, and because it is only happening in our minds, it is by definition completely imaginary.

In this case, because my client was not invited to join her friends at a gathering, she created a story that supported the judgment that she was undesirable and unwanted by her friends. In her mind's eye, she imagined her friends all together at this gathering, laughing and having a good time, while she sat at home all alone. She noticed that the scene in her mind of her friends included a bright festive atmosphere, and the one of her was dull and dreary, sitting alone in a quiet room. All of this happened quickly in her imagination, and without her practice of mindfulness, she likely wouldn't have even noticed it. This was the story she had created.

Just thinking about this sounds depressing, doesn't it? But it's easy to see how this story was entirely a figment of her imagination. This is a wonderful example of the mind's power to tell us convincing but completely untrue stories, and if we believe these stories, we suffer.

This question is also a good place to look back into your past experiences, which you discovered in the exploration practice, to find the reasons why you elected to tell yourself this particular imaginary story instead of any other one.

In my client's case, when she asked herself this question, she immediately remembered an experience from high school when she was mocked and made fun of by a group of others students when she tried to join their "clique." She experienced a huge social embarrassment at a young age and even ended up changing schools. Although this bad experience had been fifteen years earlier, it left her overly sensitive, and she recalled other times after that when she made the judgment that "no one wants to be around me." In this way, she was able to determine a possible reason for her current story.

One caveat: sometimes we are unable to pinpoint the reasons why we tell ourselves a particular story, and the good news is that knowing its origins or reasons is not necessary to release yourself from it. I can't stress this point enough. While it can certainly be helpful to know where our stories come from, sometimes you're not going to figure it out right away, if ever. This doesn't stop us from continuing on to the next step and finding out what is true for us in this moment.

Question #3: What do I know to be true?

Another thing I love about Buddhism is its focus on the present moment. The present moment is where the stories of the mind lose their power, and that is what is pointed to with this third question. This question invites you to step into the now and state only what you know. As you start looking at the "evidence" you've amassed for your negative self-talk and self-judgments, you may find that your collection of marks against yourself crumples when you confront it with the facts alone.

In my client's case, the only thing that had happened was that her friends had not asked her to join them; that's *all* she knew to be true. Everything else was a judgment and a corresponding story to support that judgment. She contrived a sad and depressing narrative that worked hand in hand with her negative self-talk, and all of it was imaginary.

She realized that the only truth was this: she had not been asked to join this gathering, and that's it. Everything else was her interpretation of the situation, likely clouded by past experiences. She was interpreting the situation to mean that she was unwanted and unlovable, but this interpretation was really based on her previous biases and had nothing to do with this situation. By focusing on the direct experience instead of the added flavorings and perceptions she'd created, she was able to stop telling herself this story, and stop suffering as a result.

This question shifts the focus onto the facts, leaving out our opinions about the situation. It also helps to ground ourselves in reality rather than running in circles of stories and getting stuck in our cycle. When I can see that the negative self-talk isn't based on truth, I can cut it free and watch it fly away like a stray balloon.

Sometimes when we ask these questions, our first reaction may be to justify all the reasons why our self-talk is true. You might hear yourself saying that people really *don't* like you and that's why they don't invite you places or that you're lazy because you haven't worked out in two days. You're irresponsible because you forgot to pay your credit card bill. You're a horrible parent because you lost your patience with your child the other day.

Answers like these come so easily to us because they "prove" the negative self-talk and back up these judgments. Here is where we have to remember to be compassionate with ourselves and look deeper at the questions. This is why we call it a practice, because it takes *practice*. The ultimate goal is to focus on the facts and not the judgments or stories. Once you can see the reality of the moment in front of you, you won't be stuck in stories that create your suffering.

When we sit and ruminate on these questions, we can also begin to untangle ourselves from past experiences, societal influences, and a mindset of scarcity. We begin to see from a new perspective that reveals not only our true nature but also that of the situation itself. Most important is that we also begin to feel better. We're no longer punishing ourselves with our imagination.

When you first begin this practice, I strongly encourage you to write out the questions and answers rather than just thinking about them. There is something about having the words on the paper (or screen) in front of you that allows you to understand, remember, and process them in a different way. When you do something in your head only, it's easy to get off track, either by forgetting a portion of your answers to the questions or having your attention hooked by something else.

Once you've asked effective questions about your judgments and found the stories that you're telling yourself, your next step is to release the negative self-talk and judgments that underlie them. This is vital in moving yourself to a balanced way of communicating with yourself, as it helps us to let go of old ideas, beliefs, and judgments that no longer serve us.

Oftentimes after answering the three questions in this practice, you may find that you begin to feel better right away. This is perfect because the last question, "What do I know to be true?," is actually the start of the release process, as you focus your mind just on the facts instead of the story, judgment, or negative self-talk.

Exercise

Question Your Own Negative Self-Talk

Remember the negative self-talk phrases that have been following you around, that you listed in your journal during a previous exercise? Now we're going to put them through the questioning practice.

Pick one recurring phrase to work with at a time. This exercise can be intense, so I would really like you to focus on them one by one. Below are some examples using very common negative self-talk issues. Notice I said very common, because it means if you are having variations of these you are not alone!

Variations of negative self-talk: *I am not successful at my job. I am not as successful as my coworker. I can't do my job right. My coworkers hate me.*

Revealing Questions	Answers
What judgment am I making?	I judge myself to be poor/ unsuccessful/failing/ somehow deficient.
What story am I telling myself as a result of this judgment?	I imagine others to have something I "need." I see them happy, with money in the bank, doing what they love. And I envision myself feeling left out, I fear I may lose my house, or not get the house that I want, or the car, or the promotion.
What do I know to be true?	I have enough money in my bank for today. I am good at my job. I am not in competition with my coworker.
Bonus question: Where does this story come from?	Belief in scarcity and belief that I need to be "the best," which I equate with having more money, stuff, etc.

Here's another example:

Negative self-talk: *I'll never find love, I am unlovable.*

Revealing Questions	Answers
What judgment am I making?	Because I am single, I judge myself to be unlovable, and that it will be this way forever.
What story am I telling myself as a result of this judgment?	I see my friends in happy relationships, and I imagine them to be happy while I imagine myself growing old alone.
What do I know to be true?	I'm not in a relationship with someone else right now, that's all. I am in a relationship with myself.
Bonus question: Where does this story come from?	Societal influences: I think I need someone else to be happy in my life. My past experience: I remember when I was in a relationship and happy, and of course, I focus on remembering the good times only, not the work that is involved or any painful moments.

Here's another example:

Negative self-talk: *I'm fat. I look horrible. I hate my body.*

Revealing Questions	Answers
What judgment am I making?	I look at my body and I judge myself to be fat and ugly, and I get angry.
What story am I telling myself as a result of this judgment?	If I am fat and ugly, no one will want to be around me. People will be embarrassed to be seen with me. I am embarrassed to be seen with me.
What do I know to be true?	I have fat on my body, but I myself am so much more than fat, so much more than my body.
Bonus question: Where does this story come from?	Societal Influences: Seeing advertising for diets and exercise rather than healthy living. In third grade I was teased for being overweight, and I have agreed with that story ever since.

Key Ideas

- Human beings are story-making creatures, and questioning the validity of the stories we are spinning can help us focus on what is true rather than getting stuck in our stories.

- When you find yourself engaged in negative self-talk, ask yourself the following three questions: What judgment am I making? What story am I telling myself as a result of this judgment? What do I know to be true?

- By continually returning to what you know to be true, you begin to untangle yourself from any unhelpful stories.

CHAPTER 7

The Practice of Releasing

Two traveling monks reached a town where there was a young woman waiting to step out of her sedan chair. The rains had made deep puddles and she couldn't step across without spoiling her silken robes. She stood there, looking very cross and impatient. She was scolding her attendants. They had nowhere to place the packages they held for her, so they couldn't help her across the puddle.

The younger monk noticed the woman, said nothing, and walked by. The older monk quickly picked her up and put her on his back, transported her across the water, and put her down on the other side. She didn't thank the older monk; she just shoved him out of the way and departed.

As they continued on their way, the young monk was brooding and preoccupied. After several hours, unable to hold his silence, he spoke out. "That woman back there was very selfish and rude, but you picked her up on your back and carried her! Then she didn't even thank you!"

"I set the woman down hours ago," the older monk replied. "Why are you still carrying her?"[6]

For many of us, the various manifestations of our negative self-talk are like heavy bags we have been carrying for many years. Like this wonderful story, the

---

6 This traditional story has been excerpted from *Zen Shorts* by Jon J. Muth, Scholastic Press, 2007.

practice of releasing negative self-talk is all about letting go of what you no longer wish to carry. Imagine the lightness you could feel by setting the burden of your negative chatter down. The truth is that you've carried it long enough.

The purpose of the releasing practice is to help you go further down the path of becoming your own best friend by setting down the burden of negative self-talk and replacing it with truthful and compassionate words instead. It is also in this practice that we will begin to use your voice in a more positive way.

In Buddhism, the opposite of release can be described as "clinging" or "attachment," a state of mind that the Buddha recognized as instrumental in causing suffering. Our goal with the practice of releasing negative self-talk is to end our suffering by ending our tendency to hold on to things or cling to that which no longer serves us. When we are attached to something, whether that is a belief, idea, person, or material possession, we will inevitably suffer.

Because most of us have difficulty releasing our negative self-talk (hence the reason for this practice), the implication is that we are actually clinging to it. This is often a revelation for people. When I tell clients that they are refusing to put down the very negative self-talk that is causing them suffering, many disagree at first. "Why would I hold on to it? I don't want that!," they often say.

One reason that we find it difficult to let go of our negative self-talk, even when we can see the fallacies of the beliefs and judgments that go underneath it, is this: negative self-talk has become a habit. Like many habits, we have done it for so long that we often just continue to do so because it's what we are used to, because it's comfortable, or even because we are unaware that it is a habit. One aspect of our release practice is recognizing negative self-talk as a habit within us, and making a conscious decision to change it.

The second reason we cling to our negative self-talk is that we have created an identity for ourselves around it. In other words, over time we have come to view ourselves as "the victim," or the "perpetrator," or the one who isn't good at relationships or with finances, or the one who needs to try harder, or the one who has failed, and so on. As a result, our negative self-talk is simply there to reinforce this identity that we have created for ourselves. One of my clients who had tortured herself with negative self-talk for years said to me, "Once I stopped beating myself up, I didn't know who I was."

So our practice of releasing negative self-talk begins by becoming willing to give up a habit and a piece of our identity. The good news is that just recognizing our negative self-talk as a habit and an identity is part of the release practice, because simple recognition helps loosen its grip on us. That's what I love about self-knowledge— when we bring something about ourselves out of the shadows and into the light, it immediately begins to change us in some small way.

Of course knowledge alone only goes so far, and we will want to combine that knowledge with action to bring its benefits to fruition. To break or lessen the power a habit has over us typically requires persistence and repetition. Reminding ourselves that negative self-talk is a habit and making a release statement are especially effective for the subtle ways we beat ourselves up (such as getting down on yourself for standing in the shower and realizing you forgot to buy soap). For example, the next time you notice that you're beating yourself up for something small or subtle, I would like you to speak these words: "This negative self-talk is a habit, and I choose to release myself from it." This little technique is surprisingly effective, and I have included a brief exercise at the end of this chapter to help you use it in your day-to-day life.

The next aspect of our release practice focuses on the larger issues we use as ammunition for our negative self-talk. These are the stories we have trouble letting go of, and in most cases they too have become a part of our identity. They also often deal with more serious issues from our past, things that we regret, or things we experienced that caused us great pain. The purpose of this next part of the release practice is especially helpful with certain areas where judgments and long-running narratives leave you feeling stuck, unable to escape the unhelpful chatter.

The Power of Forgiveness

One of the goals of the Middle Path of Self-Communication is to teach you how to speak to yourself the way you would to your best friend, not as your own biggest critic. In this way, we begin to mend our relationship with ourselves.

When it comes to mending relationships, one of the most important things one friend can do for another friend is to *forgive*. The same is true on our journey in becoming our own best friend. If we can forgive ourselves for our past actions, as well as the words we say and how we treat ourselves, releasing our negative self-talk comes much easier. Self-forgiveness is especially helpful when dealing with negative self-talk associated with regret.

Even given the benefits, for many of us forgiveness can be a daunting task—especially self-forgiveness. We often experience some resistance to this idea either because we do not think we deserve to be forgiven, or because the idea of forgiving ourselves has never occurred to us. This is why treating yourself with compassion is so important. If you spoke negatively to a friend instead of yourself, wouldn't you ask for their forgiveness?

Just like your other best friends who occasionally say something that might be hurtful, we must understand that we too can say things to ourselves that are hurtful. Most of us can understand when a friend is frustrated or stressed out—but often we do not give ourselves the same compassionate goodwill.

When our real-life friend says something hurtful, after everything has calmed down, we forgive them because we know that what they said came from a place of extreme emotion. This is exactly what we want from our self-communication and our relationship with ourselves: we want to be able to extend the same compassion and consideration to ourselves that we do to our real-life best friends.

I experienced the importance of the need to forgive myself after my first love and best friend passed away unexpectedly. After his death, I dove into workshops to try to find a way through the pain. While I learned many things to help me deal with the grief of this devastating loss, it was also here that I began a deeper journey into my own self-discovery.

At first, the more I learned about myself, the angrier I got at my parents, society, teachers, friends, and anyone else who may have influenced my negative self-talk. "If Jenny K. in the eighth grade hadn't made fun of me for doing poorly in math, maybe I would think I was smart; if my parents hadn't drummed into me the need to be frugal, then maybe I would be okay with spending money on myself without feeling guilty."

Of course, while this mindset of "blaming others" is a common reaction for many people when they first start doing inner work, it is also misplaced. While I learned more about who I was and what I wanted, I was simultaneously frustrated and annoyed at myself, because I realized that all this time I had been letting other people's ideas become my guiding principles. It wasn't Jenny K. in the eighth grade who was making me suffer (I realized the impossibility of this when someone pointed out that I hadn't spoken to her in decades), *I* was the one who was making me miserable. It wasn't my parents anymore, it was all on me. That's a huge concept to take in for someone who had spent much of her life in the mentality of a victim, and had created part of her identity out of it.

Consequently, it was not easy for me to fess up to the fact that part of being an aware adult meant that I had to take 100 percent responsibility for my own life, including how I treated myself. To let my old pattern of negative self-talk go, I had to learn to forgive the root cause of it—myself, over the many years I had neglected to communicate to myself as a friend and confidant.

I also had to look back and forgive myself for the past actions that resulted in the self-judgment and negative self-talk in the first place. Until I was able to do so, I was effectively still clinging to them. I would use these memories like a club and pull them out every so often to beat myself over the head with them. Forgiveness of my past is what allowed me to remove the poison from the wound and address the dis-ease within myself rather than just the symptomatic negative self-talk.

Finally, I realized I needed to forgive others and the situation itself too. In my own case, I found there was a correlation between what I held against others and what I held against myself. In other words, I was only able to forgive myself to the extent I could forgive others.

For some of my clients forgiving others was the more difficult proposition. If you find that is true in your case as well, please remember that forgiveness is for you, not for the other person. The purpose of forgiving is for *you* to be able to release and let go, so it really doesn't matter if the other person is repentant, deserving of forgiveness, or even knows you are forgiving them. The point is that you want to release any negativity from the situation because when you cling to this negativity you eventually use it against yourself in the form of judgment and negative self-talk.

To help you in this process, I've outlined a three-step forgiveness process that I walk my clients through when we work on releasing negative self-talk. Here is where we are going to begin consciously using our words in a more positive way. To this aim, each step includes a statement of forgiveness for you to say out loud.

This forgiveness process can be applied to all types of situations, but is particularly helpful around recurring themes and situations in your negative self-talk. As you become more familiar with the process, feel free to switch it up as not every step will apply in every instance. Remember, the goal here is to release the burdens you have been carrying for so long, and forgiveness is the key.

The three steps of forgiveness and their corresponding statements are:

1. Forgive yourself for the judgment and negative self-talk.

Think of all the ways you have spoken negatively to yourself and judged yourself around a specific situation (relationships, finances, body image, etc.). Some of my clients have actually found it helpful to write the statements they have made to themselves down on paper. Then, with all your negative self-talk and judgment in mind, say the following statement aloud:

> *I forgive myself for judging myself and for all negative self-talk that I engaged in as a result. We all say things from time to time that aren't helpful or accurate, and I forgive myself for saying those things to myself.*

Along with myself, many of my clients have found it helpful to repeat the above statement after each instance of negative self-talk. As I said earlier in the book, negative self-talk is typically not something we banish forever, but we can see huge reductions in frequency and temperament once we implement the practices on the Middle Path of Self-Communication.

2. Forgive yourself for your role in the situation.

Now let's look at the specific instances that led you to make these judgments and create negative self-talk in the first place. Think of the things you did and the things you didn't do, acknowledging any place you wished your actions were different, and accept that they are not. Remember, this is not a place for you to blame yourself for what happened. This is an opportunity for you to see your responsibility in the situation, allow, and forgive it. When you have the situation and your role in it firmly in mind, speak these words:

> *I forgive myself for _____ and all the suffering that occurred as a result. We all do things from time to time that cause suffering, and I was doing the best I knew how to do at the time.*

Forgiveness allows us to see that we were doing the best we could at the time. In the words of Maya Angelou, "When we know better, we do better." This is a mantra for us as we move forward. As with the first step, repeat this forgiveness mantra every time you find yourself embroiled in regret for your past actions.

3. Forgive others and the situation itself.

Next, think of any other people (or perhaps the situation itself) that you may be blaming for a role in your suffering. Did someone do something that was unkind or even cruel? Did you find yourself the victim of an unfair situation? With this in mind, breathe deeply and say the following aloud while thinking of the person, group, event, or situation that you have been blaming:

> *For the ways I have been harmed by you, whether knowingly or unknowingly, I forgive you. I have been carrying this pain for too long and I am putting it down now.*

Like the first two steps, forgiveness for others is not a onetime event. Many of my clients have had to return to this forgiveness process more than once for the same circumstances. It can take a while for the mind and heart to feel and believe the forgiveness you are extending to another through this process, especially if you have been abusing yourself around a certain topic for years.

I've also had people tell me that they don't feel any release after saying the forgiveness statements because they don't feel like they mean what they are saying, and that's okay too. Forgiveness is often a "fake it 'til you make it" process. In other words, when you begin to extend forgiveness to yourself and others, it may not feel real immediately, but every time you repeat the process you are breaking the old habit of clinging to the judgments and negative self-talk, and over time you will feel the peace forgiveness brings.

Forgiveness is often the most important step in the release practice, and can really be helpful in moving beyond the negative self-talk feedback loop. Extending forgiveness is also tangible evidence to ourselves that we don't want to cling to the past or our negative self-talk. Some of my clients have lived through very traumatic life events that generated years of negative self-talk. Forgiveness is what freed them, and this is evident because they are now able to talk about those life events with amazing ease. It's clear they are not controlled by them anymore. This is what I want for you.

Exercises

The Three Steps to Forgiveness

Now it's time to apply our forgiveness process with specifics. Remember these three steps are to get you started, and you may want to mix them up depending on the situation. Forgiveness is very much a "rinse and repeat" exercise, so don't be afraid to refer back to this exercise whenever it is necessary. In this case, we will use an example of judging yourself to be unworthy of love because of previous relationship failures, but this is a process you can do with any negative self-talk or judgments.

Judgment: I am unworthy of love.

1. Forgive the judgment and negative self-talk.

Think of (or write down) all the ways you have spoken to yourself around the judgment that you are "a failure" at relationships. When you are ready, make the following statement aloud: "I forgive myself for judging myself to be a failure and for any negative self-talk that I engaged in as a result. I see now that we all say things from time to time that aren't helpful or accurate, and I forgive myself for saying those things to myself."

> *Potential negative self-talk:*
>
> I am a failure with relationships.
>
> No one will ever love me because I'm a bad significant other.
>
> I'm too selfish to be in a relationship.

> *Releasing statement:*
>
> I forgive myself for judging myself to be a failure and for any negative self-talk that I engaged in as a result. I see now that we all say things from time to time that aren't helpful or accurate, and I forgive myself for saying those things to myself.

2. Forgive your role in the situation.

Now go back to the specific instances that have led you to judge yourself a "failure" in relationships. Perhaps you cheated on your partner, or weren't there for them in their time of need. When you have these examples in your mind and your role in it, speak these words: "I forgive myself for the actions I took to create this situation. I was doing my best." Next I want you to include specific language about the actions or inactions that you are forgiving yourself for. Using our examples above you would say, "I forgive myself for when I cheated on my partner. I was doing my best at the time," or "I forgive myself for not being there when my partner needed me. I was doing my best at the time." You don't need to make excuses, which our mind automatically flies to; just accept that a situation happened, you had a role in it, and that is all.

Potential roles:

> I cheated on Don.

> When Susan needed me while her mother was hospitalized, I was physically, mentally, and emotionally absent.

> I did not contribute 50-50 in my relationship with Sylvia and asked her to put in all the effort.

Releasing statements:

> I forgive myself for when I cheated on Don. I was doing my best at the time.

> I forgive myself for not being there for Susan when she needed me. I was doing my best at the time.

> I forgive myself for not contributing in my relationship with Sylvia. I was doing my best at the time.

3. Forgive others and the situation itself.

Is there anyone else that you are blaming for your "failure" in relationships? Did someone else not live up to your expectations? Breathe deeply and say aloud to the person, group, event, or situation that you struggle with, "For the ways I have been harmed by you, whether knowingly or unknowingly, I forgive you. I have been carrying this pain for too long. I forgive you." Sit with these words and draw in long, steady breaths as you feel the impact of speaking words of forgiveness out loud.

Potential others:

> I blame Don for working too much and never paying attention to me.
>
> I blame Susan for not being there for me when I was the one who needed support.
>
> I blame Sylvia for being controlling.

Releasing statement:

> For the ways I have been harmed by you, whether knowingly or unknowingly, I forgive you. I have been carrying this pain for too long. I forgive you.

Use a Code Word to Trigger a Release

Rather than saying, "This is negative self talk and I choose to release it," one of my friends says "mosquito" every time she notices herself spiraling into not-so-helpful language. I love this for two reasons. The first is that out of all the species on the planet, I still don't know what purpose mosquitoes serve. All they seem to do is annoy, irritate, cause people discomfort, and spread disease. But that's exactly what our negative self-talk does! It is annoying and irritating, it makes us feel uncomfortable, and it can be pretty dangerous. The second reason I like her reminder practice is that by saying a seemingly random word when we find ourselves spiraling out of control, we keep ourselves from falling back into the habit of negative self-talk. A code word gives us an opportunity to break from the negative self-talk and to come into a place of awareness from which we can step into the process of listening, exploring, asking questions, and releasing.

Think of your own code word to use during these situations. It can be anything, but it should be a word that you don't use too often. If you're part of a band, "trumpet" might not be a good word for you, but it might be a great word for an astronomer.

Once you have selected your word, anytime you notice yourself spiraling into negative self-talk, pull out your code word and use it as a stop sign to keep you from proceeding further down the path of negativity.

Key Ideas

- Negative self-talk can become a habit or even a part of our identity. Releasing it starts with noticing the habit and any identity we've created from it, and then becoming willing to give up this habit and identity.

- Forgiveness, of ourselves and others, is often the difference-maker when it comes to releasing our judgments and the negative self-talk that keeps us stuck.

CHAPTER 8

The Practice of Balance

In Buddhism, the ideas of balance and the Middle Path trace their roots all the way back to a man named Siddhartha, the founder of Buddhism.

Siddhartha was born a prince in the sixth century BCE, in what is now Nepal. Although he grew up in a life of extreme luxury, in his late twenties he abandoned his royal life and began a quest for enlightenment.

Renouncing his hedonistic upbringing, Siddhartha pursued the other extreme and adopted a life of austere asceticism. He abandoned all creature comforts and chose to live in the forest, taking as little sustenance as possible. It wasn't long before his physical appearance was unrecognizable, his body reduced to mere skin and bones.

But after a few years of this lifestyle, his goal of self-realization was still elusive. One day as he sat in meditation, a musician walked by and was explaining to a companion the principles of the lute (a musical instrument much like a guitar). The musician stated, "If the strings are too loose, they won't play correctly, but if the strings are too tight, they will break. It's when the strings are neither too loose nor too tight that the music is beautiful."

These simple words prompted a realization within Siddhartha: the answer to his quest could not be found in either extreme hedonism or extreme suffering. The best thing for him to do was live a life of moderation in all things. As a result, he gave up his self-inflicted torture and adopted what has become known as the Middle Path, or the desire to live a life of balance in all areas.

Similarly, the Middle Path of Self-Communication invites you to give up your own self-inflicted torture, to stop berating yourself with negative self-talk, and adopt a more balanced form of self-communication instead.

The practice of balance is the final practice in this book because, in many ways, the balance we seek is the result of doing all the other practices. When you listen to your self-talk, explore the judgments it came from, ask effective questions, and release your negative self-talk and the underlying judgments, you are already headed toward more balanced self-communication. The truth is that the more you make the other practices a part of your daily life, the less you will find yourself experiencing negative self-talk, and when it does arise, you'll find you are able to notice it and address it quickly.

Furthermore, when you don't exude the negative emotions that accompany negative self-talk, you'll likely find that your interactions with others will improve too—as will other areas of your life. For example, if you aren't frustrated with yourself, you won't inappropriately take that frustration out on others. If you don't berate yourself in your morning shower for forgetting to buy soap, your chances of having a better day improve exponentially.

At the same time, there is more to balance than just eliminating the problem. In this practice, our goal is to replace our old communication habits with new ones that reflect how we want to speak to ourselves going forward, rather than continuing the old patterns of the past.

Worst Enemy versus Best Friend

The first habit we want to give up is one we have already covered throughout this book. Many of us have spoken to ourselves in ways we would never speak to anyone else. In this way, we've acted more like our worst enemy than our best friend. This old habit is one that certainly needs replacing, and much of the work we have done in this book so far has been to that aim.

As you may have already noticed, speaking to yourself this way often does not come naturally. Most of us have many years of history around speaking to ourselves with negativity. Speaking to yourself with compassion may feel uncomfortable at first, but you'll find that over time it creates a sense of calm and connectedness within you. That's because every time you speak to yourself as a friend instead of a critic, you are choosing to give up suffering rather than create it.

In the practice of balance, we want to go further into developing self-talk that supports us as our own best friend instead of our own worst enemy. I'd like you to think for a moment about some encouraging words you might say to your best friend. Remember that for some of us our best friend may be our spouse or a member of our immediate family. Think about how you would speak to them in the morning as they head out to start their day. Perhaps you would say:

I love you and I hope you have a great day!

Remember to have fun today!

Next, I'd like you to think about what you would say to them if they were feeling stressed, frustrated, upset, or another negative emotion that was causing them to beat themselves up. Here are a couple of examples:

Take it easy on yourself, this is going to be okay.

You are doing a great job, and I love you.

There are many variations of statements you could list, and you likely can see where I am headed with this. One way you can begin to replace the old habit of being your own worst enemy with a new habit of being your own best friend is to speak those words to yourself. Doing so every morning as well as when you are feeling negative only takes a minute, but can go a long way toward changing your outlook.

For instance, before you leave the house in the morning, look at yourself in the mirror, directly into your own eyes, and say the following: "I love you and I hope you have a great day!" This can feel very awkward for many of us, but why is that? Don't we all want to love ourselves and hope that we have a good day? Many of us have no trouble speaking to ourselves the opposite way with our negative self-talk, so the reason it's uncomfortable is that we have never learned to see ourselves as our own best friend, and this practice is about changing that paradigm.

I like to mix up the words I say in the morning and add specifics for that day. "Good luck with the new book launch!" or "Have fun at the party tonight!" Learning to speak to yourself this way sets a tone for the day, and once this new habit is developed you will likely find that if you forget to do it in the morning, you miss having that extra encouragement from your biggest fan. That's good news, because like your other best friends, you miss them when you don't talk to them.

Next, when you find yourself in a moment of suffering, take the time to soothe yourself through your internal talk. Like your morning statement, this can be uncomfortable at first, but it really goes a long way toward replacing the old habit with something helpful.

Half Empty versus Half Full

Practicing balance doesn't mean you replace chronic negative self-talk with positive affirmations that aren't true for you, as doing so would simply be going to the other extreme. That doesn't mean you shouldn't choose to see positive attributes in situations. Seeing the positive can be very helpful to your overall well-being and is also an important step toward balance.

Many studies have shown that optimism rather than pessimism can lead to better health, finances, and personal relationships, and optimism is consistent with the desire to reduce or eliminate suffering.

When I ask my clients if they are a "glass-half-empty or half-full" kind of person, most of them say they are glass-half-full types. Yet when I ask them specific questions about how they see their bodies, their finances, their abilities, or their relationships, it's amazing how their sense of optimism begins to dwindle. My point is that while most people want to be optimistic or even see themselves that way, when it comes to their own self-image and resulting self-communication, this is much more of a belief than a reality. Part of our balance practice is to include optimism in our thinking and self-talk, but only to the extent that it is true for us.

For instance, the other day I was sitting with a friend who kept talking about how she's scared to have children. Her language went something like this: "I'm not going to have children, I'm afraid I will be a bad mother." As we discussed it further, I learned that her own troubled childhood had left her with a fear that she didn't know how to be a good mom and she was afraid she would repeat the mistakes of her own mother. It was also apparent that she had been holding on to this fear for many years.

When it came to motherhood, she was seeing her future as half empty rather than half full. As we talked further, I suggested she might consider a more balanced observational approach instead, one that included the possibility of an optimistic outcome. Perhaps her self-communication could go something like this: "I didn't have a great example of motherhood growing up, but if I choose to have children, I will do my best to get educated and be the best mom I can be. " As soon as she began to even contemplate this idea, I could immediately sense a positive change in her mood.

My friend may have children later in life or she may not, but whatever she decides, my hope is her decision won't be the result of judgment, fear, and the accompanying negative self-talk. Equally important is the fact that by replacing her old habit of judgment and negative self-talk with a balanced observation and optimistic language, she has reduced her suffering around this issue right now.

Judgment versus Observation

Since judgment is at the root of all our negative self-talk, our next step toward replacing an old habit with a new one addresses this directly. While acknowledging that the mind has a habit of judging, is there another habit we can develop instead? In my experience the answer is yes, and it is what I refer to as observation. Judgment is loaded with things like comparison, expectation, assumption, and the other catchphrases and buzzwords of the seven negative expressions we covered earlier in the book, while the latter is grounded in neutrality and facts.

Let's look at a couple of examples between judgment and observation so you can truly see that there is a difference, even though our minds would sometimes claim the opposite. We will start with an example as it relates to others in the world and then move on to ourselves.

Imagine I have a family member who has borrowed money from me previously and not paid it back. If they ask to borrow money again, I could speak about the situation in two ways:

> **Judgment:** I can't believe he would ask to borrow money from me again; he hasn't even paid me back from the last time. He needs to get a job and get his financial house in order. He is pathetic. I'll tell him no.

> **Observation:** He has borrowed money from me before and has not yet paid it back. I don't think it would be wise, based on past experience, to loan him money again. I'll tell him no.

One narrative is true, helpful, and kind; the other is full of ideas about right and wrong, good and bad, and includes my demands about what another person "should" do. The judgment perpetuates suffering, and the observation comes from a place of neutrality. It's also important to note that the action taken—not loaning the money—is the end result in both cases.

Now let's look at another example, but this time applied to an area where negative self-talk is extremely common: body image.

Let's say I am standing in front of the mirror looking at my body just after coming home from an annual physical where the doctor raised concerns about my weight as it relates to my long-term health.

Judgment: I am so fat! Even the doctor said so! How embarrassing! I have got to get my butt to the gym and start eating right. But it's so hard, I'm not sure I can do it, I shouldn't even waste my time trying.

Observation: The doctor said overall I am in good health, but that he is a little concerned about my weight. He said if I began to exercise and eat better, I would likely lose ten to fifteen pounds, have more energy as a result, and be less susceptible to things like diabetes and heart disease as I get older. Changing my diet and adding exercise is tough, but I think I can do it.

Here again, the observation is true, helpful, and kind. The judgment is the opposite; it's a cacophony of negativity. Also, notice how the language of the judgment not only perpetuates suffering, but it also impacts the action I plan to take.

Understanding the difference between an observation and judgment and making an effort to speak to yourself in a way that reflects neutral observation rather than negative judgment are a big step toward replacing an old habit with a new one.

Bringing Observational Language and a Positive Outlook Together

Now let's combine the last two lessons. Earlier in this book we covered seven common expressions we use to speak negatively to ourselves, each with their own buzzwords and catchphrases. We learned that these expressions are always tied to a judgment, so let's look at some examples of how these expressions might be shifted to include an observation instead. You'll see that the new language we can substitute into these expressions is consistent with balanced communication. Our goal is to develop new habits that include balanced observations in our self-communication and look to the positive when appropriate.

Replace Overreaction with Calm and Balanced Assessments

Earlier in the book I mentioned a client of mine who had been trying to eliminate sugar from her diet, but after eating several pieces of candy on Halloween, she reacted by telling herself: "I totally blew it. There's no point in trying to diet now."

How might a balanced, calm assessment of this situation look instead?

Perhaps my client could have said to herself, "In hindsight, eating all of that candy probably wasn't a great decision, but it is Halloween, and I can get back on track starting right now."

Developing a habit of calm and balanced assessment rather than an overreaction can also greatly improve your communication with others. For instance, most of us have been in a situation where someone exaggerated a problem in a negative way, and that is never helpful.

> **The switch:** To make the switch from overreaction to balanced assessment, you will focus on what's true and make a calm observation instead.

> **Old habit:** "That was the worst mistake I could ever make," or "Everything is terrible."

> **New habit:** "That wasn't my best. Next time, I will do better."

Replace Personalization with Balanced Responsibility

Previously I mentioned a client who blamed herself and her divorce for all of her teenage daughter's problems. In this situation, a balanced sense of responsibility might look something like, "I know the divorce has been difficult for her. I am here to help as much as I can, but any action she takes is her own."

Determining what is our rightful responsibility in a situation can be difficult sometimes, but it is always more helpful to bring a spirit of observation rather than judgment. When it comes to relationships, oftentimes you may find you have far less responsibility than your old habit of negative self-talk suggests. As I mentioned earlier in the book, the truth is that others are responsible for their own choices, just as we are responsible for ours.

> **The switch:** When we come from a place of observation, we acknowledge any role we have in a situation, but nothing further.

> **Old habit:** "It's all my fault," or "I'm to blame for this."

> **New habit:** "I played a part in this situation. I am doing my best and am only responsible for my own decisions and actions."

Replace Absolute Language with Balanced, Relative Language

The problem with absolute language is that it leaves no room to be more than one thing. If you say "I am not a happy person," then you can't be happy even for a moment, or you risk losing your whole identity. When we replace it with relative language such as "I am not happy *right now,*" we leave room to change and aren't held captive by absolutes.

Switching from absolute to balanced, relative language also applies to blanket statements we make about our abilities and ourselves. For instance, "I'm bad at math" becomes "Math isn't my strongest subject." This is a small difference, but can pay dividends in how you feel over time.

> **The switch:** You are much more than any one thing. Rather than ascribing a single quality to yourself and making it "who you are," bring an observational perspective to yourself and how you feel.

> **Old habit:** "I am fat."

> **New habit:** "I have fat on my body, but the size of my body does not determine who I am as a person."

Replace Assumption with Focus on Facts (And Not Knowing!)

This is where your observation skills can really be tested, as the mind's attachment to the old habit of assumption is strong. The key to loosening its grip is to focus on the facts in any situation and to be cognizant of any story that the mind wants to create around the facts. The truth is that in the vast majority of cases we simply don't know the intentions behind other people's actions or inactions.

In Zen Buddhism, there is actually a practice called "don't know mind" (or alternatively "beginner's mind") where the focus of the practice is to simply become comfortable with "not knowing." When we think we know something, we close ourselves off to learning something new, to exploring other possibilities. Not knowing opens us in new and exciting ways. When it comes to assumptions, adopting a "don't know" mind-set allows us to put down the burden of trying to guess or interpret any meaning or significance of what other people are doing or thinking.

Lastly, when you do make an assumption, here is another area we can lean towards the positive. Many people already practice this—they call it giving someone "the benefit of the doubt," meaning that if you don't know what they are thinking/feeling, you might as well assume the best rather than the worst, if you're going to assume at all.

The switch: You can't know what anyone else is feeling or thinking. What you do know are the simple facts in front of you.

Old habit: "They didn't say hello to me, that means they don't like me."

New habit: "They didn't say hello to me. All that means is that they did not say hello to me; nothing more or less. Maybe they didn't see me."

Replace Expectation with Open Curiosity

Like assumptions, expectations are another deeply ingrained and often subtle habit of the mind. When it comes to their being a source of negative self-talk, they are largely fueled by what are otherwise positive goals we don't reach in the way we think we should. "I should be married by now," or "I should have that job," or "I should be a better Buddhist."

The implication of this way of thinking is that what we are right now isn't good enough.

A friend of mine has a practice that I love. When he notices his mind react based on an expectation, he asks himself the following question: "Why is this better than what I had planned?" In this way, he is looking for the gifts that arise in situations where he initially didn't get what he wanted. "Why is not being married right now better than being married?"

The switch: Let go of the need to control the situation, and allow reality to be as it is. Enjoy whatever comes up!

Old habit: "This isn't how it's supposed to be!"

New habit: "This isn't what I was expecting, but how exciting is it to try something new! I love surprises!"

Replace Comparison with Cooperation and Sympathetic Joy

Much of the habit of comparison is rooted in societal ideas about what is important and the concept of scarcity. If you look closely, you'll find that the things we typically compare to others are often based on the values given to us by outside sources. Who defines what attractiveness is? How does one define intelligence? Why are wealth and the acquisition of material possessions important? The next time you catch yourself comparing, see if you can find the origin of your measuring stick.

Instead of comparing, shift your focus to observing any differences between you and others and celebrate their uniqueness as well as your own.

Buddhism has a practice that addresses the habit of comparison directly. The practice of mudita, or sympathetic joy, is where you choose to consciously celebrate the accomplishments of another. In other words, choose to be happy for the other person without using their accomplishments as a means for self-deprecation. This is not an easy practice to say the least, but it's also one that is a big step away from the self-created suffering that comes when we compare.

The switch: Instead of viewing life as a competition, view it as cooperation.

Old habit: "They are smarter/more attractive/ wealthier than I am."

New habit: "They are doing so well! I love to see others prosper; there is enough good in the world for us all."

Replace Regret with Appreciation

We've seen in many examples how the old habit of regret is extremely powerful fuel for negative self-talk. For those of you who struggle with regret, this new habit might seem radical, and before you undertake it, I strongly encourage you to stick with the practice of forgiveness outlined in the previous chapter (for yourself, others, and the situation).

Even after we begin to experience some of the release associated with forgiveness, feelings of regret can still be hard to shake. To help you do so, I suggest you make a list of good things that have come from the same event or situation you regret. This doesn't mean you chose that event or situation, or that you wouldn't do something differently if you could, it just means that you acknowledge that it happened, and you recognize the perennial truth that good things also come from these tough life occurrences.

There's an old adage that "behind every gray cloud is a silver lining," which means that even bad situations can have unexpected benefits. Our task here, along with continuing down the path of forgiveness, is to look for the unexpected benefits, even if it takes years to uncover them.

> **The switch:** Instead of holding on to old judgments about situations, try to see the benefits that the situation brought to you.

> **Old habit:** "If only that hadn't happened . . ."

> **New habit:** "If that hadn't happened, I never would have met . . . / never would have experienced . . . / never would have seen . . . etc. I'm grateful for that experience, which I used to regret."

The above examples are just a few of the ways in which you can shift your language and replace old expressive habits with new ones. The key is to move from judgment to observation, and to focus on the positive when it is appropriate to do so. Remember, our goal is to speak to ourselves in a way that is true, kind, and helpful, and changing these habits can help us do just that.

Meditation

Returning to the story of Siddhartha for a moment, it's important to note that while the realization of pursuing balance in all things was an important one, it alone did not lead to enlightenment.

For this Siddhartha went and sat under a bodhi tree to meditate, vowing not to get up until he could understand the nature of reality. It was here, through meditation, that Siddhartha finally realized his goal, and this is what earned him the title we know him by today.

When he got up from this meditation, he was altogether changed, and that change was noticeable to his companions. As soon as they saw him, they asked the question, "What happened to you?" Siddhartha replied, "I am awake." The word for "awake" in the Pali language of the day is *Buddha*.

As a result of this, no practice is more important to Buddhism than meditation. For our purposes, I have found that developing a habit of regular meditation is critical to our practice of balance. One aspect of meditation includes observation, as you learn to witness your thoughts rather than attach to them, and this is exactly what we want to do with our negative self-talk.

As you know by now, all forms of negative self-talk have something in common: they are based on the belief that there is something wrong with you. Buddhism actually says the opposite. There is no problem with you, your suffering is the result of habits of the mind, and meditation is the primary way that Buddhism suggests you can undo these habits. The proof offered by the Buddha that this is so was his own enlightenment, as he ended his own suffering through meditation.

Unlike many prescriptions for your mental health, meditation is unique because it implies that you already have everything you need inside you—there is nothing outside of yourself that is necessary for you to be complete or to be fixed. Because of this, any self-talk that says you aren't enough *can't be right.*

You may or may not believe this, but just acknowledging that it is possible is a step toward balance. As a certified meditation instructor and communication expert, I can attest that the practice of balance is greatly enhanced by regular meditation. Through it we begin to calm the mind, moving away from habits that lead us around like an untamed horse to develop a centered presence instead.

There are entire books written on meditation and how to do it, and many of you reading this are likely already familiar with meditation. For those of you who are not, I have included exercises to get you started.

Exercises

Starting a Mediation Practice[7]

If you are new to meditation, below are some simple instructions to get you started.

Find a quiet place where you can be alone for a few minutes without distraction.

Sit on a cushion with your legs crossed and your knees below your hips, or sit on a chair with your feet firmly planted on the ground, hands resting on your thighs. You want to sit up straight, assuming an upright posture, and your gaze should be about six inches in front of you. You may also close your eyes if you prefer. Although you're sitting tall, you don't want to force the position; it should be comfortable. Once you're in position, take a couple breaths and focus your attention on your breath to bring you into the present moment.

The easiest way to begin is to keep your focus on your breath, concentrating on the inhale and then the exhale. When your mind starts wandering, simply note that you're thinking, and bring your attention back to your breath.

Many first-time meditations go something like this: You close your eyes and start thinking, *Okay, focus on my breath . . . inhale . . . exhale . . . I need to send that*

---

7 This exercise is based on one that appears in my previous book, *How to Communicate Like a Buddhist,* which contains additional meditation techniques as well.

e-mail . . . inhale . . . exhale . . . I forgot to put food in the
dog bowl—wait, did I put the food in the dog bowl . . .

As you focus on your breath, your mind may spin with minor explosions of thoughts about things, people, ideas, and feelings. All of this can leave you thinking, "Oh no, I'm doing this wrong," but the truth is that this is what happens to the vast majority of us. What you want to do is simply notice the thoughts as they come up, and then gently turn your attention back to your breath. The moment you notice you're following a story or line of thought, that's your cue to come back to your breath. What this teaches us is how to observe our thoughts without becoming consumed by or attached to them. Start slowly, doing this for five or ten minutes, and gradually work up to longer periods of time. It helps if you can find an instructor or group to meditate with, as there is something about doing this with others that makes it easier on all of us.

Learning to Laugh

Finally, in our efforts to practice balance and replace old habits with new ones, let us not forget the importance of learning to laugh at ourselves when appropriate, or simply to not take ourselves too seriously. For many of us, laughter comes naturally when we don't take our negative self-talk too seriously. This is especially true for many of the little ways we chastise ourselves.

For instance, standing in the shower and realizing we forgot to buy soap could be a moment of comedy and laughter rather than suffering and self-flagellation. Rather than saying to yourself, "How could I be so stupid?," perhaps you can chuckle at your mistake instead.

Learning to laugh at yourself is a sign of friendship, as friends often laugh with each other. You may even notice that many of us who have adopted severe self-criticism are also out of balance when it comes to what is serious and what isn't. A quick question I ask myself to try to decide what's serious and what's getting amped up in my brain is simply, "How important is this?" "Is this smoke from a wildfire or a barbecue?"

This may seem like a small change, but finding the humor in life is a fabulous way to eliminate suffering. It's very hard to belly laugh and be miserable at the same time.

Key Ideas

- The Middle Path means living between extremes, in a state of balance. The Middle Path of Self-Communication means living between the extremes of negativity and false positivity, always looking to express truth.

- Observations are a straightforward account of the facts, while judgments are colored with our preferences.

- Balance occurs when we replace our judgments with observations.

Afterword

Change Your Words, Change Your World

As we near the end of this book, I want to acknowledge that in the deeper understandings of Buddhist doctrine, the advice "talk to yourself like a Buddhist" would have little meaning, because perhaps the greatest realization the Buddha had in meditation is that the self we are talking to doesn't exist in the way we think it does— this is called the Buddhist doctrine of annata.

But until that is true for us on an individual basis, negative self-talk is a source of suffering, and learning to love yourself rather than criticize yourself lessens this suffering.

In my own case, as I prepared for this book, I looked back at my journals from when I was younger, well before I started discovering this process. What I saw was astonishing. From this distant perspective, I saw how I had created an exorbitant amount of suffering in my life through my negative self-talk. The language I was using even in my journals was harmful and unhelpful. I wrote things like "I should be over this by now" and "I'm too emotional, this isn't how normal people handle their emotions." My negative self-talk was manifesting not just in my internal monologue or soliloquy, but through my writing as well.

But you see, when I started paying attention to how I was speaking to myself and the root judgments that were causing my negative self-talk, I saw how I was perpetuating the thoughts and feelings I didn't want through the very language I was using on myself. I was caught in a cycle of dissatisfaction, anxiety, and fear, and once I understood the pattern that was creating my dissatisfaction, I could see how to move beyond it.

The amazing thing I realized is this: how we talk to ourselves defines how we view the world, and we have the power, at any moment, to change this. To enjoy our lives, to really see that the world is full of possibilities rather than liabilities, we need to let go of the negative self-talk and speak to ourselves from a place of compassion, aware of any self-judgments and biases that arise, and replace them with truthful, helpful, and kind language.

When I changed how I communicated with myself, the rest of my world began to change too. That's because the negative self-talk I was putting myself through cast a dark cloud over my day and my perceptions of others and the world, often without me even realizing it.

What I have also learned is that the Middle Path of Self-Communication is an ongoing process. As I mentioned earlier in the book, it's unlikely there will be a day when you "defeat" negative self-talk once and for all, as making judgments and the corresponding negative self-talk are part of the human condition. The good news is that you now have practices by which to examine these judgments, so that you don't believe everything you think without question.

I don't think of negative self-talk as a bad thing anymore, in the same way that I don't necessarily think of a sneeze or a cough as particularly bad. They're symptoms of other issues. Our negative self-talk is an indicator that judgments are happening, and like sneezes or coughs, they could be indicators of small and insignificant judgments, or more serious ones that I need to look at more deeply. In this way, I'm grateful to my negative self-talk, because it shows me where I need to work next.

Moving Forward in Your Self-Communication Journey

By using the five practices that we've discussed in this book, we can develop a type of self-talk that comes from a place of honesty, compassion, and love. When we talk to ourselves from a place of kindness, we can move past our old judgments and the suffering they cause us in our everyday lives. When we can see that what we've been saying to ourselves all these years isn't actually the truth, that's when real shifts begin. It isn't easy to continue to speak to yourself from balance, and it will require you to repeatedly check in and go through the five-step process over and over again, especially in the early stages of your self-communication journey, but the more you practice the steps of the Middle Path of Self-Communication, the easier you'll find balance.

At this point, you have all five practices that can help you let go of your negative self-talk and start interacting with yourself in a more helpful and balanced way. Each practice is something you can do when you notice negative self-talk by picking apart each phrase (or focusing on one that has been rattling you for a while) and taking it through the process.

Hopefully you aren't feeling overwhelmed by the processes and information I've shared in this book, but if you are, I'd like to leave you with a few final words of encouragement, in case your negative self-talk is rallying itself to tell you that it's all too hard.

There is a reason why we call the lists of activities at the end of each chapter "exercises." Weak muscles find any type of exercise difficult, but over time they build up strength and soon exercises that seemed hard aren't difficult at all. Your self-communication is the same way—until now it hasn't been getting a good workout, and negative self-talk and judgment can run rampant, but as you start these workouts, these *exercises*, it will grow stronger. It will be easier to become aware of your negative self-talk, to identify the underlying judgments, to explore and question them, and release them on your way to balance. As your communication muscle develops, you will be able to see negative self-talk as it comes up, address the underlying issues, and find your way back to balance more quickly.

It's okay to stumble. It's okay to backtrack. This is only natural when you're building a new muscle and learning a new skill, but the one thing I'd like you to take from this book is this: If your words are causing you suffering, the good news is that you can change them. And when you change your words, you change your world.

Acknowledgments

It's been a joy for me to work on this book and to share my experience with you. What I love most about this journey is helping others apply and implement these practices in their lives. I am extremely grateful to those who have let me in and trusted this process to help change their days. It is your openness to a new way of interacting with yourself that has enhanced and improved my work. Thank you to I.L.N. and S.S. for your constant support throughout the writing process, to my parents and sis who have been my biggest fans since day one, and to my mother and father-in-law whose interest in my work makes me feel so loved. Having been pregnant while writing this book, I am truly grateful for the team at Hierophant Publishing. Their flexibility and patience during this time made me feel supported, and their guidance and skill in turning my work into a finished product is quite masterful. Lastly, I want to thank my husband and little baby love; their presences inspire me and remind me daily of my desire to live in a way that is kind, honest, and helpful —I weird you both big-time.

About the Author

Cynthia Kane is a certified meditation and mindfulness instructor who received her BA from Bard College and her MFA from Sarah Lawrence College. Her work has appeared in numerous publications, including the *Washington Post, Chicago Tribune, Yoga Journal,* and *Woman's Day Magazine.* She is the author of *How to Communicate Like a Buddhist* and the founder of the Intentional Communication Institute. She has helped thousands of people change their way of communicating through her online courses, workshops, and certification program. She lives in Washington, DC with her husband and son. Visit her at www.cynthiakane.com.

Also by Cynthia Kane:

Available wherever books are sold.

Hierophant Publishing
8301 Broadway, Suite 219
San Antonio, TX 78209
888-800-4240

www.hierophantpublishing.com